Path of the Golden Teacher

For the online course and live meditation classes & events
with Sean McNamara
visit
www.WisdomWithin.space/PathOfTheGoldenTeacher.com

Also by the author

Renegade Mystic is also available in audiobook format.

Also by the author

Mind Sight II

TELEPATHY TRAINING for Neurotypicals

THE ESTES PARK SESSIONS

SEAN MCNAMARA

Also by the author

Note: The simplest growing method is included here in *Path of the Golden Teacher*. The book pictured above offers several methods, using over 300 photos to guide you step-by-step.

Yinyang with psilocybin mushroom spore prints

Yinyang represents the universal balance of opposites such as light and dark, creation and destruction, etc. These forces flow into each other in a naturally perpetuating cycle of transformation.

Journeys with psilocybin and other psychedelics have the potential to transform this philosophical concept into a genuine, deeply felt understanding in the core of one's being. This drastically shifts one's perspective of reality and offers profound meaning, inspiration, and resolution.

Dharmachakra mudra with mushroom

In Buddhism, the Dharmachakra mudra represents the "turning of the wheel" (chakra) of the teachings (dharma). The Path of the Golden Teacher is **not** Buddhist, though there are similarities. This is a universal approach, applicable by anyone regardless of their spiritual, philosophical, or religious affiliation.

In our context, the mudra represents the union of profound knowledge and special techniques. Meditation training is both, it's a set of techniques and the revelation of knowledge. The psychedelic journey is the second stage of this path. It reveals knowledge usually hidden from ordinary consciousness by drawing on the insights gained through the first stage (meditation) then going much, much deeper.

After the journey, the meditator may resume daily practice as a form of integration and familiarization. Or they might simply resume ordinary day-to-day activity, even without meditation, while viewing life through a new lens.

It's important to note that these meditations are effective even without their combination with psychedelics. They can still alter one's perspective of life and reality.

Companion to the Online Meditation Program

This book is intended as a companion to the online video-based guided meditation program by the same name, *Path of the Golden Teacher*.

However, **many people will find the book helpful even without using the online program**, especially if they already have a well-established meditation regimen.

This meditation program is not affiliated with any religion or group. However, some of the techniques (not all) will be familiar to Buddhists since the author spent many years training in one of its many lineages.

He no longer identifies with any religion or organization. There is no expectation that you would replace your current belief system or religion. If you already have a path, you'll find a way to apply the information in this book to it.

Practical, experiential, and free of dogma, he teaches without using poetic "fluff," magical thinking, or confusing non-English terms. The online program is comprised of over 50 instructional videos for you to watch during formal meditation sessions. They progressively lead to more subtle and profound states of awareness. Maturity and patience are necessary to proceed on this path fruitfully.

Whether or not you use psychedelics, this path is substantial enough to be practiced for the rest of your life.

Find the online program at either of the following sites and use the **coupon code** "goldenteacherbook" at checkout for a significant price reduction. The discount can only be applied at time of purchase. It cannot be applied retroactively.

www.WisdomWithin.**space**/PathOfTheGoldenTeacher

or www.PathOfTheGoldenTeacher.com

Path of the Golden Teacher

Integrating
MEDITATION
with
PSILOCYBIN
and other
psychedelics

Sean McNamara

Mind Possible Publishing

Copyright © 2024 by Sean McNamara

All cover and interior images were created by Sean McNamara unless otherwise credited.

All rights reserved. No part of this publication may be reproduced or distributed by any means without the author's written permission.

Published by Mind Possible

ISBN: 979-8-9883119-4-2

DISCLOSURE AND RELEASE OF LIABILITY

This book does not offer medical advice. It is intended as a harm-reduction resource.

The reader should consult their physician and do further research before using any substance mentioned herein.

Psychedelics have a range of risks. Some are well-known. Others have yet to be identified. A list of contraindications has been included here but it is impossible to predict every possible outcome from using a psychedelic.

Meditation also has a range of risks. Like psychedelics, some are better known than others. A list of contraindications for meditation has also been included but it is impossible to predict every possible negative outcome from meditating.

As such, the author does not blanketly recommend psychedelics or meditation because that consideration should be done on a case-by-case basis according to an individual's needs, strengths, and risks. It is assumed the reader has already decided to experience meditation or psychedelics or is using this book to help with their decision-making.

If you follow the guidance or instructions in this book or its accompanying online guided meditation program, you do so at your own risk and release the author, his associates, and heirs of all liabilities and accept full responsibility for your actions.

TABLE OF CONTENTS

Acknowledgments   i

INTRODUCTION

The Ancient Way   2
My Experience   7
Your Experience   23

PART ONE: THIS PATH OF MEDITATION

Introduction to This Path   28
Contraindications for Meditation   49
Meditation as a Protective Measure   53
Integration Meditation   65
Solitary Meditation Retreat Practice   69
Solitary Retreats with Psilocybin   78
Group Events with the Author   79
Support for Challenging Meditation Experiences   81
Suggested Progression   82
    The Foundational Series   87
    The Cognitive Series   91
    The Heart Series   94
    The Transpersonal Series   99
    The Space and Energy Series   101
    The Deep Peace Series   104
    The Nature of Mind Series   110
    The Visionary Series   117
    The Sleep and Dream Series   117
    Meditation on the External Elements   117
    Union Practice/Sexual Yoga   117

PART TWO: THE PSYCHEDELIC JOURNEY

Introduction to the Psychedelic Journey	120
Contraindications for Psychedelics	123
Support for Challenging Psychedelic Experiences	129
Cautionary Tales	130
How to Journey Alone and Why	140
Preparation	147
Your Journey	164
Integration	172
How to Journey with a Sitter	176

PART THREE: GROWING AND USING PSILOCYBIN

Introduction to Growing	187
Materials and Equipment	190
Equipment for Harvesting and Storage	192
General Timeline from Start to Harvest	193
Detailed Instructions for Growing	194
Dealing with Mold	208
Introduction to Microdosing	210
How Determine Your Ideal Microdose	216
How to Test for Potency	220
Using a Digital Scale for Measuring Dosage	223
How to Consume Your Microdose	224
Your Microdosing Schedule	226
Daily Microdosing Journal	228
How to Determine Your Ideal Journey Dose	230
How to Consume Your Journey Dose	236
Boosting Your Journey	238
Better Than Ayahuasca or Peyote	240

PART FOUR: CANNABIS & DMT

Cannabis with Meditation and Psilocybin	243
Journeying with DMT	258
How to Extract DMT	261

How to Use DMT   294
My Journey with DMT   302

PART FIVE: FINAL CHAPTERS

Reviews From the First Meditators   308
Reference Images for the Visionary Series   313
Conclusion   320
How to Submit a Review   322
About the Author   323

ACKNOWLEDGMENTS

I want to begin by thanking Jill Lowy, Cheryl Macchia, Neal Clegg, Dana Baggs, and Celal Aydemir. You were the first ones to use the online program. We also spent several months meditating together over Zoom and in person. You took a chance on me, and your feedback has been invaluable. I cherish the time we shared, and it gave me the confidence to offer this path to the public.

I must acknowledge that I didn't invent any of the meditation techniques presented in the online program. I've merely adapted what I learned from my teachers who received the practices from their teachers and so on for many generations.

No matter the circumstances under which we parted, I'm still grateful for the good times we shared, the lessons you taught me, and your practice instructions. I hope I repay your efforts by passing your wisdom to the next generation.

I also want to acknowledge the person without whom none of this work would have been possible, María Sabina Magdalena García[1]. In 1955, the Mazatec healer and spiritual guide generously allowed the Western ethnomycologist Gordon Wasson to participate in a ceremony with her that included psilocybin mushrooms. He wrote about his experiences and published his work for the world to read.

As industrialized people of colonialist nations, we must never forget the original wisdom-keepers who have held and protected deep knowledge of healing, spirituality, and consciousness since time immemorial.

---

[1] Gordon Wasson used the pseudonym "Eva Mendez" in the famous May 1959 Life Magazine article *Seeking the Magic Mushroom* to hide Sabina's identity.

Acknowledgments

We haven't discovered anything. We've only recently experienced things those wisdom keepers already knew about, and we've mislabeled our ideas as breakthroughs. For us, it's as if something doesn't exist unless it's been approved by the ivory tower's gatekeepers and published in academic papers and scientific journals, which just isn't true.

Maria Sabina, thank you. And I'm sorry. Your contribution to the world came at too high a cost to you and your family. This must not be forgotten.

Finally, I wish to thank my wife. Cierra, you've always supported my journeying, and you were always there when I needed a shoulder to cry on. Your presence, feedback, and insights continue to influence my sitting, my writing, and how I train others. I couldn't have done this without you.

INTRODUCTION

THE ANCIENT WAY

    This is an open path. It is also our birthright as conscious beings. Since people are diverse in their ways of thinking, beliefs, and existential needs, this path cannot, and must not, be hemmed in by religious dogma or political control.

    I begin this way because sharing my narrative requires me to refer to my prior experience as a Buddhist practitioner, which I am no longer.

    This is not a Buddhist book, nor a Buddhist path. I stopped identifying myself as a Buddhist or as a member of any religion many years ago. Please don't interpret my statement to say everyone should abandon their religion. If yours works for you, great.

    I am not anti-Buddhism or anti-religion. But I am against harm, abuse, and neglect by people in any spiritual, political, academic, professional, or familial position of power. When any person or tradition limits or prevents your use of nature's resources for exploring your mind, it's not only harmful but also violates your inherent right as a conscious being.[2]

I hope you'll benefit from this book regardless of your religious affiliation. And if you're non-religious, an atheist, or agnostic, you're also welcome.

This book is primarily intended as a companion to the online guided meditation program by the same name, *Path of the Golden Teacher*.[3] Please understand the "golden teacher" is not a person. It's the name of a popular strain of the Psilocybe cubensis mushroom often recommended to new cultivators and users.

But this is just a name, a label, a marketing tool. Other strains can be used for this path, of course. And other types of psychedelics can be included as well, either grown in the earth or created in the lab.

The meditations and their order are designed to offer exceptional preparation for a psychedelic journey. They're also valuable for post-journey integration. They can transform what might only be an entertaining experience into one granting the most profound understanding of the nature of reality. They also support healing and transformation.

If you are curious about the types of meditations that comprise this path, you can find the complete list in the chapter *Suggested Progression* in Part One. Some of these practices will seem familiar to practitioners of the completion stage practices of Mahamudra and Dzogchen such as thogal and karmamudra. But this is not that.

To be clear, I am **not** teaching Buddhism here, and these practices are not to be examined in that context or compared to it. They are different. Of course, it's possible for different paths to lead to the same mountaintop.

---

[2] Of course, we must balance personal rights with our obligation to not harm others through our actions. This is why responsible, informed use matters.

[3] Find it at www.WisdomWithin.**space**/PathOfTheGoldenTeacher and use the coupon code "goldenteacherbook" (no spaces) for a discount.

The Ancient Way

Based on my personal experience, psychedelic journeys preceded by ample training in meditation are an effective route to that peak. Meditation not only helps us integrate the knowledge gained, but it also helps us retain our insights long after we've hiked down the trail and returned to the village. And we must come down. We can't stay up there forever, no matter how we arrived.

After creating the online meditation program, I realized these techniques offer a complete path even without the use of psychedelics.

Therefore, **you don't need to use psychedelics to benefit from the meditations** in the online program.

And you don't need to use meditation to obtain at least some benefit from psychedelics.

You may already be committed to a daily meditation practice as part of your religious or spiritual affiliation and would prefer not to replace it with the one offered here. That's perfectly fine.

The choice is yours, and you should respect your intuition and preferences above anyone else's, including mine. I hope this book serves as a helpful complement to whatever spiritual path you've chosen for yourself.

Part One will help you reflect on the role, limitations, and risks of meditation. It will also offer ways to integrate meditation into your psychedelic process.

Part Two will prepare you to have a psychedelic journey by yourself or with the help of a trusted friend. While the medical and pharmaceutical industries would have us look to them as the best providers of psychedelic services, they are costly and have their risks and limitations.

Another advertised resource for psychedelic healing is the shamanic experience. The term "shaman" is highly problematic in certain contexts because of cultural appropriation, questions of authenticity, misrepresentation, price gouging, and harm done to vulnerable cultures in Central and South America due to psychedelic tourism.

Plus, not everyone seeking to journey is interested in adopting the use of language, music, ritual, prayer, and metaphysical concepts that do not align with their established worldview.

This book offers self-empowerment by showing how to provide for your own psychedelic experience. You don't need to give your autonomy away, pay outrageous sums of money, or adopt an exotic belief system to have a complete experience.

Part Three will teach you how to grow, store, and consume psilocybin mushrooms. It will also teach you how to microdose and how to determine your ideal dose for journeying alone, safely.

There are other types of psychedelics, for example, LSD, that can be used with this meditation path. But trustworthy sources of LSD are hard to find, so Part Four includes information about another psychedelic which is far easier to acquire than LSD, dimethyltryptamine (DMT). It includes step-by-step instructions for extracting and vaporizing crystallized DMT in the privacy and comfort of your home.

Also, Part Four discusses using cannabis and psilocybin synergistically, and how to use cannabis alone for meditation.

This is an open path, but that doesn't mean everyone will be open to it or that it's even appropriate for them. Part One describes contraindications for meditation, and Part Two does the same for psychedelics. But still, who is this book and its optional accompanying online meditation program really for?

When I envision you, the reader, I see someone fiercely determined to answer their spiritual questions themselves instead of being told what to believe.

Believing for belief's sake isn't good enough for you. Dusty books and dry philosophy leave you wanting.

The Ancient Way

You seek real experiences instead of taking things on faith. You're also mature and independent enough to go your own way while others question your loyalty to their group, their beliefs, and their power dynamics.

You're ready to reclaim any personal power you've given away, intentionally or not, to external authority figures. You're done asking for someone else's permission or a special blessing to look at your own mind.

You might also be at the end of your rope, disappointed by unfulfilled promises and frustrated by the existential threats your religious leaders or spiritual teachers pose when you doubt, question, or challenge them.

Maybe you've been hurt and are ready to start healing. Perhaps you need a fresh start, a new path free of the triggering language, concepts, and symbols that remind you of the teacher, group, or tradition you needed to leave.

What matters most is that you're driven to pursue a spiritual discipline in a meaningful way. You're ready to apply yourself consistently. This is good because the path offered through this book and the online program is not necessarily easy and it isn't fast.

It requires you to make the time and space in your daily life to practice meditation for at least forty-five minutes a day most days of the week if every day isn't possible. In the modern age, certain people have become accustomed to quick, effortless gratification. They wouldn't like this path.

There are no shortcuts. There's no background music and no electronic brainwave manipulation because what we seek is the unconditioned mind, pristine awareness.

There are no secrets here, and no levels for comparing yourself to anybody else. Nobody gets a title, special name, or certificate at the end. There are no rituals, no robes. No selfies either, no showing off, because there's nothing to see. This is between you and your mind. How far you go is solely up to you and there are no guarantees.

This is the ancient way.

MY EXPERIENCE

    I was nervous. Sitting across the room was an ordinary-looking white guy in his fifties. He wore a button-down shirt, slacks, and tennis shoes. He looked straight ahead but wasn't focusing on anything. The room was dead quiet. Something special was about to happen.

    His back was close to the wall. Behind him hung a large *thangka*, a Tibetan tapestry depicting Padmasambhava, the man who brought Vajrayana Buddhism from India to Tibet in the 8th century. Today, many Himalayan Buddhists regard him as their root guru. The thangka was the only thing that indicated the spiritual nature of this event.

    There were about a dozen of us, seated on chairs in a semi-circle so we could all have a clear view of this man. Just for this single event, someone had rented the conference room inside a hotel in Borrego Springs, a small tourist town located in the middle of southern California's Anza-Borrego State Park.

    The desert outside had been blisteringly hot earlier that day. But it was evening now, and the air-conditioning felt refreshing. But I was still sweating.

My Experience

I didn't know this man, and I didn't know anybody else there either, except for Andrew, my childhood friend who'd invited me on this trip after I expressed interest in learning how to meditate.

Andrew, the others, and the oddly staring man in the front of the room were all students of an American self-proclaimed Buddhist master. He had become a wealthy and controversial guru to thousands of followers before his untimely and mysterious death in the '90s.

But I didn't know about any of that at the time. I'd flown from Colorado to spend a few days learning how to meditate. I was a blank slate. And I quickly realized this wasn't a beginner's meditation class. I was about to receive what they called the *pointing-out instruction*, pointing out the true nature of mind.

Earlier, someone told me that the pointing-out instruction was a powerful opportunity to glimpse the enlightened mind, and if my karma was ripe for it, to even become enlightened myself. I had no background information about this, no preparation, and no basis for comparison. But I wanted to believe, and that made me vulnerable.

I'd already stopped going to Mass on Sundays. My family was Catholic, and there have been times in my life when I took the faith seriously. But I was in my early twenties now, and for a variety of reasons had become dissatisfied by being told what to believe. I was too stubborn, curious, and critical to rely on faith alone.

Now, I sought real experience. I wanted to learn to meditate so I could answer my questions about the mind, the body, and what happens after we die. I'd lived with persistent anxiety about death since the third grade when a ruptured appendix nearly killed me.

I hoped meditation could show me a deeper reality. Perhaps I could experience something that made me unafraid to die by showing that something in us endures. And maybe it would stop the sleepless nights lying in cold sweat, staring at the ceiling while imagining my ultimate oblivion.

So, here I sat, still sweating but for different reasons. "Could this be it?" I wondered. "Is this what I've been looking for?"

We must've sat there for a half-hour, but I didn't dare lift my wrist to look at my watch. Nobody moved, and nobody spoke. Supposedly, we were meditating. But I didn't know how to do that yet, so I simply waited. It felt a little like sitting in church. And then it began.

The man slowly raised his hand until it was level with his head. Everyone's eyes fixated on him. The whole room felt tense, and nobody breathed.

He snapped his fingers, just once, then slowly lowered his hand. Nobody spoke.

"Was that it?" I wondered. I didn't feel anything. I didn't see anything special. And my mind...it was the same as it was before the finger snap.

I turned my head as slowly as possible so I could see how the others were reacting without being noticed. Some appeared to meditate. Others were smiling. "I must've gotten it wrong. I must've missed it," I thought.

I don't remember most of what happened the rest of the time we were in that room. He told us not to overthink it, and we were not to discuss it with each other. Talking was thinking, and thinking was not what this was about. In my naivete, I accepted his logic.

The next night was even more strange. After dinner at the hotel, we piled into several SUVs and were driven into the desert. The all-wheel-drive vehicles were necessary to traverse the miles of sand and rock beneath the moonlight. We went to a special place their teacher had deemed a *power spot*.

We spent an hour or so sitting on the edge of a dried riverbed while the leader reminisced about being with his master. Years ago, at that very same spot, he witnessed his

My Experience

guru levitating a couple of feet above the sand.[4] This was only one of several paranormal tales he shared with us.

After the storytelling was finished, it was time for another pointing-out. One of his assistants lined us up while he situated himself twenty yards away. One by one, we were instructed to approach the teacher slowly and stop right in front of him. He'd tell us what to do when we got there.

From my position in line, I could see each person in front walk toward him. But it was too dark to see what happened once they got there. Yet, I could vaguely see each one return to the cars after a few moments with the teacher.

It was my turn. "What the hell am I doing?" I wondered. It was all starting to feel contrived. Half of me was inspired by the teacher's miraculous stories and the other half regretted paying the airfare. I walked into the darkness toward the oddly staring man.

When I reached him, I noticed he was looking directly into my eyes. It wasn't aggressive, but direct. Without saying a word, he reached out and grabbed my shoulder as if to steady me.

Suddenly, he pounded the palm of his other hand into the center of my chest. It didn't hurt, but it caught me off guard. Later, someone would tell me this type of pointing-out involved the heart chakra. We silently stared at each other for a moment before he released me. "Now go back to the car but don't talk to anyone. Just look at your mind."

I did as he said, but it was already clear to me that nothing special had happened. I was a bit in shock from being struck in the chest without warning, and the melodrama of the evening added to my feeling awkward. But I hadn't become

---

[4] Many years later, I watched a documentary about the leader and cult dynamics. It explained how peer pressure and heightened expectation can cause a person to imagine seeing these types of phenomena, and that it was a type of psychologically-produced hallucination. Based on that and other information, I don't believe the man actually levitated.

enlightened. I hadn't had a revelation. I was still the same and still afraid to die.

But I didn't give up. After returning home, I looked up several meditation centers near me. After visiting a couple, I settled on one rooted in a Vajrayana (Tibetan Buddhist) lineage. I met people there who, I'm grateful to say, actually taught me how to meditate. I felt an instant connection with them and their teachings.

I was also drawn to the meditation center's appearance. Thangkas hung on every wall. They depicted historical figures as well as otherworldly beings and elaborate mandalas. Gray whisps of incense smoke stretched across the room as rows of motionless meditators breathed peacefully. I can still remember the enchanting aroma that permeated the space.

It wasn't very long before my assigned meditation instructor offered an overview of "the path" in her tradition. She said if I wanted to, I could fulfill certain requirements to qualify me to study the advanced, secret practices not available to the public. The requirements included taking several vows, meditating regularly, and attending long retreats led by senior teachers and, eventually, the guru, also referred to as the tantric master.

At that level, she told me, I would be on the *fast path*. From this lineage's perspective, not all Buddhist teachings were alike. With some, it could take millions of years before achieving enlightenment. With others, seven lifetimes. But in this lineage, if I received and practiced the highest teachings, I could achieve liberation in this very lifetime.

That was all I needed to hear. I dove in headfirst.

Over the years, I took the vows, meditated regularly, and studied the teachings. I was so committed to my spiritual development that I quit various jobs to attend month-long retreats since they were prerequisites for the secret teachings.

At the time, I prioritized that tradition and the practice of meditation above everything else in my life. I'd regret it eventually, but not yet.

My Experience

Over several years, I became qualified for the preparatory stage of advanced practices. Once again, I found myself in a room full of strangers waiting for something special to happen. But this time, there were over a hundred people in the room. Instead of a single thangka, there were many, as well as a special throne on a raised platform for the guru to sit on.

As part of our introduction to this stage of practice, he was going to give us the pointing-out instructions, just like the guy in Borrego Springs did several years earlier.

This was an elaborate ceremony that included chanting, bowing, and even prostrating our bodies on the floor in a show of reverence for the teacher and as an act of purification.

At a certain point, we approached the guru's throne so he could pour liquid into our palms for us to drink. The liquid was called *amrita*, a Sanskrit word meaning "deathless nectar," or "elixir of immortality." But it was just watered-down liquor. We were instructed to notice our minds when we drank it.

I didn't notice a thing, though. Not even a buzz.

Then came the pointing-out instruction. The procedure, though more elaborate, was pretty much the same as what happened in Borrego Springs. It had the same effect.

Nothing.

"If you didn't see it, that's a good thing," they said afterward. "And if you think you got it, you didn't." These and other platitudes were offered by the team of teachers and meditation instructors whenever someone privately admitted to doubting anything happened.

At the time, I eagerly accepted their explanation because it assured me that I was still on the right track. We spent the rest of the evening celebrating. Publicly, we agreed that something special had happened. But privately, I think more than a few of us were disappointed.

Over the years, I meditated more, attended more retreats, and did what I needed to finally receive the special practices that promised enlightenment in one lifetime.

Just like before, there was chanting, bowing, prostrating, incense, and a throne. But now there was also the playing of hand drums and bells, as well as visualizing ourselves and each other as deities in a sacred world that, like Schrödinger's cat, both existed and didn't exist at the same time.

And, just like before, there was the amrita, the mysterious fluid imbued with the guru's blessing that would reveal the part of us that was beyond life and death, beyond good and bad, and beyond coming and going. But again, nothing happened. The only thing I got from drinking the amrita was a bitter taste in my mouth.

Nevertheless, I practiced my new meditation, the "secret" one I'd been initiated into by the guru. The daily practice included drinking several drops of amrita. The ritual had been passed down through centuries from teacher to student, so I wasn't about to omit it. The good Catholic boy in me was still sheepish about challenging tradition.

But eventually, I just stopped. I stopped everything.

The guru took advantage of his power differential and had an inappropriate relationship with someone close to me. Eventually, it came out that he'd done this kind of thing with several female students over the years. It broke my trust in him and in much of what he represented.

I had another teacher too. He'd initiated me in the same practices as the other. And his amrita was just as ineffective. He also abused his power over his students, albeit differently than the other teacher.[5] I'd had enough.

I came to realize how ineffective the rituals, symbols, elaborate visualizations, prostrations, mantra recitations,

---

[5] For the details, see my other book *Renegade Mystic: The Pursuit of Spiritual Freedom Through Consciousness Exploration*. They're too difficult for me to recount here, and unnecessary for the purpose of this book.

My Experience

special breathing techniques, and ceremonious drinking of amrita had been for me. It's not that I wasn't getting anything out of my daily meditation practice and from going on retreats. I was. But it was nothing like what was described by the teachers and their ancient texts.

I knew that as a modern person whose life was filled with work, family, friends, and various distractions, it wasn't likely that I'd achieve the ultimate goal. But I still expected something more than what these elaborate practices were producing. That's when I left.

I wish to be clear here and state that I'm only commenting on my experience, nobody else's. These methods might work for other practitioners, or maybe they work better for people from the cultures in which these practices originated. I only mean to describe my results, not to blanketly criticize an entire lineage or the tradition it upholds.

For a long time, meditation was too painful because it triggered the memories of what happened with my teachers. But over time, I resumed a steady meditation practice, albeit using techniques devoid of rituals, chanting, or anything I might associate with them and the tradition I'd left behind.

I also realized that during the time I identified myself as a Buddhist, I never progressed in answering my original question about death and what happens afterward.

Like other religions, Buddhism has its dogma regarding those topics. I studied it voraciously. But what I studied were concepts and explanations. It wasn't experiential. So, this approach was not too different from the faith-based path of my childhood.

Over the years, I'd learned a lot about the tradition and its practices. But I also forgot the reason I'd gotten involved in the first place. I'd abandoned my specific line of inquiry and became a good follower instead.

I decided to refocus on my original death question. To do so, I bought books on how to have out-of-body experiences, a phenomenon I'd been aware of since watching the 1987 TV series *Out on a Limb* featuring Shirley MacLaine, who wrote the book the series was based on.[6]

The episode that affected me the most showed MacLaine (she played herself) relaxing in a natural hot spring high in the Peruvian Andes. At one point, her consciousness separated from her body and floated into outer space.

Seeing that made me wonder if I could have an out-of-body experience, and if that would finally answer my lifelong question about whether some part of me will continue after I die.

Using techniques from books, I trained every day for several months until I had my first conscious out-of-body experience. Afterward, my lifelong death anxiety was gone. Vanished.[7]

I continued practicing the techniques and having more OBEs (out-of-body experiences). During that time, I realized two important points.

First, I was able to achieve the OBE simply by learning the techniques from a book and practicing them regularly.

Second, I didn't need to receive a guru's blessing, ask his permission, become "qualified," or pay thousands of dollars to attend long retreats to have my OBE. All I needed was the instructions, persistence, and patience to keep training until it happened.

This gave me the courage to say goodbye to my teacher and his community, stop the ritualized meditations I'd devoted several years to, and drop my religious affiliation.

I shifted my focus to a type of consciousness exploration that offered real experience but without the dogma - parapsychology and psychic phenomena.

---

[6] As of this book's release, *Out on a Limb* can be watched on YouTube on various channels. Using the search term "Shirley MacLaine out on a limb out of body experience astral projection" will yield results featuring that scene.

[7] The details of my out-of-body experiences and the instructions for how to have them are in the second edition of my book *Renegade Mystic: The Pursuit of Spiritual Freedom Through Consciousness Exploration.*

My Experience

It felt like the wild west. There weren't any rules about what I could or couldn't do, and nobody was watching anyway. Over the next few years, I learned telekinesis, clairvoyance, and telepathy. These are abilities that can be tested and measured. I appreciated their verifiability because the last thing I wanted to do was fool myself. This was especially important because I eventually began teaching others how to develop their abilities.[8]

Some people, especially religious types, regard psychic abilities as parlor tricks. But I don't. They're a part of my spiritual path because what makes psychic phenomena possible is our interconnectedness on physical and non-physical planes. These phenomena provide real evidence for what is usually regarded as "woo-woo."

I credit my meditation training with giving me the capacity to develop these abilities. In some cases, the techniques involve mindfulness, though I don't necessarily call it that. Regardless, psychic development is indeed a form of mind training. It is meditation.

In 2022, something happened that would once again shift the course of my spiritual path.

I created a study to determine whether psychedelics could enhance one's psychic ability.[9] I recruited seven friends, some of whom would microdose psilocybin and Amanita muscaria. The others formed the substance-free control group.

Every week for six months, all the participants took several ESP tests including various types of clairvoyance and telepathy. After six months, I would compare the control group's performance to that of the microdosers.

---

[8] See my website www.MindPossible.com for my other books, online courses, and events related to psychic development.

[9] The details of the study, including photos of the ESP targets and the participant's transcripts, are captured in my book *Dewdrops of Infinity: Psychedelics, Psychic Abilities, UFOs, and the Puharich project.*

I included myself in the experimental group, microdosing the two different types of mushrooms. I was so focused on the ESP tests that I was surprised when I began to experience the cognitive and emotional benefits of microdosing often mentioned in the media.

About five or six weeks into taking a small dose of psilocybin four days a week, I realized I was different. It felt as if someone had lifted a hundred-pound blanket of darkness from my shoulders. For the first time, probably since childhood, I felt happiness as my baseline state. And the constant anxiety I'd lived with for much of my life (aside from my fear of death) was almost completely gone.

The thing is, I wasn't even aware that I'd been depressed. I thought the way I'd felt every day for years was normal. But after talking to others about it, I realized what I felt wasn't normal. Even though my OBE had removed my death anxiety, it hadn't removed my general anxiety. But taking a minuscule amount of powdered mushroom with breakfast for a couple of months had done just that.

I also noticed my memory was improving. The year before, I'd noticed it was getting harder for me to remember where I parked my car when grocery shopping. After buying my food, I'd exit the store and strain to remember where the car was. Sometimes I'd walk through the parking lot just hoping to bump into it.

But after microdosing for a couple of months, my memory was back to normal. It became easy to recall where I parked. I didn't even have to try. Whether it was the effect of stress reduction or something else doesn't matter to me.

After the group study was over, I realized I had an opportunity I couldn't pass up. I wondered, "What if I took large doses of psychedelics and took the same ESP tests? How would that affect my psychic perception?"

But I was nervous about taking large doses because the only time I'd done that was in college. Back then, I had no idea how to use psychedelics properly.

My Experience

On my nineteenth birthday, a classmate gifted me with a bag of dried mushrooms which I slapped into a peanut butter and jelly sandwich before going to a festival on campus. I didn't know anything about dosing, duration, mindset, setting, or the potential physical and mental effects. I was clueless. And I paid the price for my ignorance with a bad trip.

But now, almost three decades later, I was prepared. Over six months, I took hallucinogenic doses of psilocybin, Amanita muscaria, LSD, LSA, and DMT. I credit my years of meditation training for having the fortitude to take the ESP tests while tripping out. It was challenging to stay on task. After completing the tests, I would lie down either on my couch or in bed and enjoy what remained of the journey.

During one of these journeys, something I'd hoped for during my years practicing Vajrayana Buddhism finally happened. I experienced what the ancient texts described as the fruition of the path. I experienced emptiness, non-duality, and the sacredness and purity of everything in the universe.[10]

These weren't mere ideas. They were no longer concepts taken from a book. This was gnosis, produced from direct experience. As such, it was beyond words.

For that reason, I won't even attempt to describe what I saw, felt, and intuited during that journey. The understanding I achieved cannot be conveyed using language.

I also won't describe my experience because I don't want to plant ideas in your head. Your journey should be uninfluenced by mine or anybody else's. The worst thing would be for you to have a beautiful, revelatory journey but be disappointed because you didn't experience some of the same things I or other journeyers might describe.

But I should mention that my experience was absent of traditional Buddhist symbolism, imagery, or language. So, I

---

[10] If you are a Vajrayana practitioner, you will understand it if I say that during my journey, I finally realized the inner meaning of seeing oneself as the yidam, the world as the mandala, and all beings as also being the yidam. I experienced primordial purity and spontaneous presence beyond concept.

believe what I experienced was universal, something available to people regardless of their religious affiliation.

I think it confirms the notion that the view from the mountaintop is the same no matter what path each person takes. Spiritual techniques are not the same thing as the result. The path is not the view.

I realized my experience was made possible by the years I'd spent meditating. All that time, I'd been preparing for my psychedelic journey without knowing it. If my practice of meditation sowed the seed and grew the plant, the psychedelic was what caused the flower to finally bloom.

Naturally, the experience didn't last. By the next morning, I was back to my old self. But there was an afterglow that lasted a couple of days, and I was sad to see it fade. I'd finally experienced a state that teachers and traditions around the world have described for millennia, and I didn't want it to end.

But it did. Thanks to my prior meditation training, I knew I needed to, and could, let it go. It wasn't a complete loss, though. I could still recollect the message, the essential meaning of what I experienced.

To be clear, no, I'm not enlightened, awakened, or whatever words people use to describe that kind of thing, and that's fine with me. I'm okay just as I am, which was made poignantly clear during that journey.

Other journeys have yielded similar experiences. But I don't feel a need to chase after them. I got the message the first time.[11]

More importantly, those experiences reinvigorated my interest in meditation. Today, it keeps me in touch with the deeper part of me that holds the understanding gained during my psychedelic journeys.

---

[11] I also had an important experience using DMT, which I describe in the chapter *My Journey with DMT* at the end of Part Four.

My Experience

Put simply, meditation is how I remember the point of it all. It's also how I release myself when I get stuck in unhelpful patterns of thinking and acting.

And although I still train people in developing their psychic abilities, I've lost interest in developing my own. Another lesson from my journeys is that it's enough to be a regular human being. In fact, it's the best. To have this aging body with all its limitations is a precious gift. The struggle to live, connect, experience meaning, and then die is what makes it all meaningful.

Everything, and I mean *everything*, is sacred already. But these are just words on a page. Knowing it in your bones is different from reading. Psychedelics combined with meditation make that kind of knowing possible.

After these experiences, I began an online search to see what other people thought about spiritual development aided by psychedelics. Soon enough, I found several interviews with a teacher of Tibetan Buddhism named Lama Mike Crowley.

The interviews were about his books:

Secret Drugs of Buddhism: Psychedelic Sacraments and the Origins of the Vajrayana

Psychedelic Buddhism: A User's Guide to Traditions, Symbols, and Ceremonies.

Listening to him and reading his books confirmed my experience. Crowley is a translator of ancient Buddhist languages who has carefully studied traditional liturgies and symbolism. His general thesis is that psychedelics were historically integral to Vajrayana Buddhist (and pre-Buddhist) practices.

As an aside, some readers may also be interested to know of the following books about psychedelics in other religions and historical periods. Interviews with the authors are easily found on YouTube as well.

The Psychedelic Gospels: The Secret History of Hallucinogens in Christianity by Jerry Brown PhD and Julie Brown MA

The Immortality Key: The Secret History of the Religion with No Name by Brian C. Muraresku

The Chemical Muse: Drug Use and the Roots of Western Civilization by D.C.A. Hillman, PhD.

According to Lama Mike Crowley, amrita in its original form was indeed a psychedelic. Which psychedelic it was is in question since it probably depended on what was locally available during certain periods. It's also possible amrita was a combination of substances in some cases.

As I heard him explain this, I thought, "No wonder the amrita I'd drank during all those initiations and rituals never did more than leave a bitter taste in my mouth." It had only been a symbol of the real thing.

Imbuing symbolic amrita with the guru's so-called blessing simply wasn't enough to shift one's perception. But drinking psilocybin tea or taking LSD or other psychedelics can certainly do that. It did for me, even though it had been years since I stopped identifying as a Buddhist and doing their rituals.

The potential accumulated from years of meditation was still there, inside of me. And taking a psychedelic actualized it.

I still respect Buddhism today. But for a variety of reasons, I'm not interested in rejoining that or any other religion. For some people, but not everyone, religion and its very human leaders are more likely to limit that individual's spiritual development than to help it flourish.

My Experience

Meditation, however, remains my main access point for peace, reflection, insight, and re-opening my heart when it feels shut down. And meditation can be practiced independently of religious dogma.

Therefore, inspired by the work of Lama Mike Crowley and by my experiences with meditation and psychedelics, I decided to create the Path of the Golden Teacher.

The online guided meditation program teaches meditation without religious or dogmatic overlay. It includes nearly fifty meditations presented in a graduated manner for a lifetime of practice. And you don't have to use psychedelics to benefit from it. The chapter *Suggested Progression* in Part One offers a complete list of the techniques.

You'll notice the absence of rituals, mantras, prayers, music, or symbolism. Make no mistake, though. This is a powerful set of practices if applied properly. In other traditions with similar meditations, you'd need the teacher's approval and permission to do them. That's not the case here. When designing the program, I avoided creating the power differential typical in other student-teacher relationships.

For those who would like to use psychedelics as part of this path, I've included all the necessary information. This includes how to grow psilocybin, how to microdose, how to journey, how to choose (or be) a sitter, how to be safe with all of it, and much more.

No matter how you decide to proceed, I wish you the best. And if you don't proceed at all, that's alright too. You're already a sacred aspect of this ever-evolving universe. If you don't mind me saying, you are enough just as you are. If not now, I hope you know it someday. Know it in your bones.

YOUR EXPERIENCE

How you experience this book will partly be determined by your current beliefs, values, and biases. My intention is not to change them.

If any of the information here is valuable for you, then good. If it's not, then ignore it. This book should not be regarded as dogma.

It will challenge some people's belief systems, though. For example, some Buddhists interpret the fifth precept, the one prohibiting intoxicants, to mean psychedelics are not allowed and should be categorized with alcohol.

They define intoxicants as a substances that cloud the mind, cause confusion, and prevent insight into the nature of reality. And if they're addictive, they give rise to habitual clinging and grasping.

But psychedelics, though radically altering the mind for several hours, can result in profound realizations during the experience and increased clarity of mind afterward. Also, psilocybin, LSD, and DMT are not physically addictive.

Your Experience

So, no, psychedelics should not be categorized with alcohol.

And, as Lama Michael Crowley has said in some of his interviews, some contemporary Buddhist teachers are open to using psychedelics and they encourage their students to do so if it's appropriate for them in a proper, ritualized context.

What about the spiritual teachings on non-harm and compassion included in many religions? If a person has the potential to heal from depression, anxiety, and trauma by using psilocybin instead of taking a pharmaceutical drug with damaging side effects, isn't it harmful and uncompassionate to prevent them from doing so?

What does your religion have to say about psychedelics? What did your parents tell you about them? What do your friends think? And what do your preferred news outlets, political leaders, and podcasters have to say?

Our opinions are not entirely our own because our personality is highly influenced by the words and actions of the people who matter to us. If you find yourself reacting strongly, either positively or negatively, while reading this book, you might look within and identify from whom you adopted your opinion.

You might also inquire if it feels safe for you to think and act differently. It might not, and that's an important consideration.

It takes strength and courage for someone to go their own way even when they fear potential ostracism from their social group. It's a legitimate risk.

Right now, scientific research is revealing the potential psychological benefits of psychedelics. This is starting to undo the damage begun by the Nixon administration and the media in the nineteen seventies. But some people won't consider the new data, preferring to rely on what others tell them to believe.

What you believe is up to you.

But psychedelics do come with risks, are not a cure-all, and should definitely be avoided by certain people. This is why I included contraindications and cautionary tales. I expect that some people will write negative reviews without even reading the book, saying it blindly pushes psychedelics or that psychedelics have no place in spiritual practice.

Others will go the opposite direction, potentially calling it a fear-mongering, anti-psychedelic publication.

I hope those who do read the book in its entirety see that it offers a balanced view.

The same thing can be said about meditation. It comes with risks that are still not disclosed as much as they should be in other books, online, and at meditation retreats. Therefore, I've also included contraindications for meditation and its potential risks.

If you write a review (and I hope you do), it will help potential readers to know some details of your experience.

Did you read it and stop there? Did you practice the meditation techniques from the online program, or did you practice other kinds of meditation? Did you use a psychedelic in this context? If so, how? What was the result?

What was your bias before reading it? Where you for or against psychedelics? And were you for or against meditation?

If the book was helpful for you, please describe how when you write your review. Even just two or three sentences are enough. For the book to succeed and reach those who need it the most, honest and informative reviews will be essential. Our spiritual freedom and individual rights are always in the balance.

I thank you in advance.

Your Experience

Pictured below are tantric Buddhist implements including a ritualistic skull cup for serving amrita, which these days is typically watered-down liquor. Here the amrita is in the form of dried psilocybin mushrooms which can be eaten whole or ground into powder and made into a tea. Unlike symbolic amrita, psychedelics induce a radical change in perspective, making them true elixirs.

Is it possible other religions have also substituted psychedelics with mundane substances like bread and wine in modern-day rituals?

When these religions first started, small groups of people would have used psychedelics secretly to avoid public outcry. As they attracted more followers, it would have become increasingly difficult to avoid the attention, criticism, and persecution by the government and other groups.

It would have also become more difficult to source enough of the psychedelic for increasing numbers of followers, thus forcing the use of a symbolic substitute.

PART ONE

THIS PATH OF MEDITATION

INTRODUCTION TO THIS PATH

    Why do you meditate? Or if you're a beginner, what do you hope for? Peace? Wisdom? To be more loving? Or something deeper, like understanding the fundamental nature of mind and reality?

    Or maybe you're already a user of psychedelics and want to explore them in a more contemplative or spiritual context. Perhaps you've already used psychedelics for inner peace, wisdom, and a tender heart and want to go deeper.

    But you likely have other reasons for meditating, like stress reduction or to counteract the modern speediness of life. Maybe you're unhappy or feel existential dread.

    Whatever your reasons are, you might want to write them down and review them from time to time. If you also decide to have a psychedelic journey, your intentions for doing so may overlap with your reasons for meditating.

    You should occasionally compare the techniques you use to the goals you wish to accomplish and check that they're in alignment.

As I mentioned in the previous chapter, it was a long time before I realized I'd forgotten my original reason to meditate. I absorbed myself in that tradition's teachings and values, following their prescribed path instead of meeting my unique needs. I assume you wouldn't want that to happen to you.

The meditation path offered here doesn't include a philosophical base. I'm not interested in telling anybody what to think. Your values, ethics, and spiritual beliefs are up to you. Hopefully, these techniques leave room for your unique line of inquiry and exploration without compromise.

Still, there is a specific purpose and progression to this path's meditations.

The Foundational series is designed to introduce the basic technique of sitting upright and stabilizing your mental attention. This series offers more profound benefits, as well.

You'll become familiar with how the background of your mind functions and how you respond to life on a moment-by-moment basis. You'll also develop the ability to let go, reducing the stress and tension in your mind and body.

The Cognitive series builds on the foundation by helping you identify automated responses and attitudes you apply in meditation as well as in regular life. These meditations will help you reverse those responses to improve your state of mind.

The Heart series is designed to increase your awareness of emotions in your mind and body. It also helps you cultivate love and appreciation for yourself and others. On another level, these techniques teach you self-efficacy, that you can directly influence your state of mind.

Many of us have gone through life passively responding to outside influences. These meditations show us that we can be proactive and shift our mindset from within.

The Transpersonal series takes us beyond our individuality and helps us recall our interconnectedness with the universe. For those for whom this fits into their belief

Introduction to this Path

system, it also includes a practice for connecting with people who have passed away.

The Space and Energy series offers a deeper experience into our sense of self. We normally regard ourselves as physical beings, as bodies with solid boundaries. But through modern physics, we understand that solid matter isn't solid at all.

We used to think everything could be broken down into atoms. But now scientists know atoms aren't the end-all-be-all and looking more closely using instruments like the Large Hadron Collider, they find only blips of energy popping into and out of existence.

Similarly, when we use meditation to closely observe the self, we discover that on one hand, there's nothing solid there. And on the other hand, that nothingness is imbued with the everchanging presence of energy. *Energy* can be interpreted differently, so in this context, it is best to define it as *perceived experience*. Therefore, within the nothingness, there is perceived experience. But experience is not a thing, it's not single (or multiple, necessarily), it's inconsistent, and it's impermanent.

There are many insights to be gained from the Space and Energy series. Most practically, perhaps, is the realization that we are not who we see in the mirror. With time, this makes life's challenges like loss, aging, and dying easier to come to terms with.

Psychedelic journeys also reveal we're not who we normally think we are. The body can feel quite different. And glancing in the bathroom mirror at the right moment can give us a perspective of ourselves without our usual filters and judgments.

The Deep Peace series is an extension of the Foundational series. Whether you're interested in basic stress reduction or would like to experience what's left when your conscious mental activity, thought patterns, reactivity, and personality are significantly muted, these practices will help you experience that.

The Nature of Mind series uses the stability and focus developed in the previous series for investigating and differentiating the aspects of experience that make you "you."

Just as you did in the Space and Energy series, you'll discover the ephemerality of your thoughts, feeling responses, emotions, sense perceptions, and even the elemental qualities of your body. You'll also learn to differentiate your thoughts from the base awareness from which they arise.

Meditators skilled in Space and Energy techniques can apply them while hallucinating during their journeys. The hallucinations comprise another category of mind to be investigated and differentiated from fundamental awareness.

In meditation and while journeying, you will realize the cliché, "You are not your thoughts." Converting this cute bumper-sticker saying into a lived experience greatly enriches one's life.

The Visionary series is special and relies on strong familiarity with the Nature of Mind series. Cultures around the world have learned that by observing light, for example, the sun, sky, or even a candle, in a particular way, you can produce a variety of visual effects.

For some cultures, this gave the seer the ability to learn about non-human entities and illnesses.[12] In the Bön and Dzogchen traditions of Tibet, yogis use these techniques to realize the fundamental nature of their minds and bodies.

The rare but increasingly famous indication of success using these practices is for the practitioner's body to shrink into a miniature form or even dissolve into light altogether. This is known as the *rainbow body*.[13]

---

[12] Herrera, Cesar E. G. (2018). Microbes and Other Shamanic Beings. Palgrave Macmillan.

[13] To learn more about the rainbow body, many texts and YouTube videos are publicly available. It should **not** be confused by its use in New Age circles or other metaphysical groups promoting "rainbow body activation" online.

Introduction to this Path

Spiritual neophytes might hear of the rainbow body and say, "That's amazing! *I* want to do *that*!" But what they don't realize is the prerequisite for this level of realization is an understanding of the true nature of "I." When a meditator produces a rainbow body upon their dissolution, the "I" doesn't exist anymore, at least not the way it does for ordinary people.

The purpose of teaching the Visionary series here is not to help you attain the rainbow body. If that's what you want, you should find a teacher who can guide you and be prepared to abandon life as you know it and live in a secluded retreat from now until the day you die. That's what it takes, it's said.

Rather, training in the visions here adds a level of subtlety to developing stability, concentration, and realizing the nature of mind. The visions behave as a sort of biofeedback mechanism because you can't experience them very well when you're distracted.

The visions improve as your meditation improves. In this way, the visions exemplify the definition of psychedelic:

To find it in the context of Bön and Dzogchen, search using the terms "togal" and "thogal." Those with a Judeo-Christian background might enjoy Francis V. Tiso's book, *Rainbow Body and Resurrection: Spiritual Attainment, the Dissolution of the Material Body, and the Case of Khenpo A Chö*.

For those interested in an overview of Tibetan Buddhist practices including togal, I highly recommend Ian A. Baker's book, *Tibetan Yoga: Principles and Practices*. The abundant collection of beautiful photographs, art, and illustrations set it apart from other books on the same topic.

Those seriously interested in studying togal should also read Flavio A. Geisshuesler's book *Tibetan Sky-Gazing Meditation and the Pre-History of Great Perfection Buddhism: The Skullward Leap Technique and the Quest for Vitality*. As of the time of this publication, it's available to read online for free at www.BloomsburyCollections.com.

I also recommend Christopher Hatchell's *Naked Seeing: The Great Perfection, The Wheel of Time, and Visionary Buddhism in Renaissance Tibet*.

mind-revealing. And the visions do have a lovely psychedelic quality to them because of the beautifully shimmering light phenomena that arise.

As I discuss while teaching this technique in the online program, the perception of light inside one's body, whether in daylight or pitch dark, has profound implications about the nature of one's being.

The Sleep and Dream meditations differ from what is often taught for lucid dreaming and dream yoga. Here, you will learn to explore the meditating mind on the edge of sleep and have insights that change your understanding of self, thoughts, and awareness.

The External Elements series will teach you to meditate with earth, wind, water, and fire as another approach to self-understanding and transformation. The techniques are quite simple but rely on a firm foundation of the previous series of meditations.

Union Practice/Sexual Yoga will teach you how to use various states of arousal and climax to deepen your understanding of the non-physical aspects of self. This will heavily rely on your proficiency with the techniques in the Space and Energy, Nature of Mind, and External Elements series.

These practices can be accomplished alone or with a partner. And like anything else, they are optional. If you are put off by the idea of using sexual feelings for spiritual or psychological development, then of course, don't do them.

But if you do decide to do them, understand that sexual yoga (as it's presented here) is meditation first and sex second. Improving your sex life or using it to attract a lover should not be your motivation. These techniques are exceedingly difficult to practice, requiring extreme sensitivity and the capacity for delayed gratification.

And to be frank, they're not very sexy. Most of the action happens in the mind. This isn't Hollywood-style sex and it's definitely not the Kama Sutra.

Introduction to this Path

However, these techniques have the potential to heighten your experiences of concentration, stability, space, and energy.

All the meditations in the *Path of the Golden Teacher* can benefit your psychedelic journey. The chapter *Meditation as a Protective Measure* explains how, generally, meditation supports resiliency during the experience.

Some of the meditations are specifically designed to prepare you for what might come up. For example, the Heart series includes practices for facing someone who hurt you in the past. During a journey, it's possible to encounter that person or someone similar, which can be unsettling, to say the least.

Preparing for this situation during meditation converts an event that would normally be avoided into an opportunity for healing and transformation.

Intensive meditation isn't for everyone, though. It comes with psychological and physical risks that everyone should be aware of.

I remember a friend I introduced meditation to when we were in our mid-twenties. One day, I taught him a basic technique of following the breath. Two years passed before I heard from him again. When I did, he told me how, one day while meditating, he became hyper-focused. He'd had a psychotic break. His mother came to visit and found him scrubbing his kitchen floor inch by inch using a toothbrush. She took him to the hospital where he spent several months in psychiatric care.

When I taught him the meditation, I didn't know he already had a history of mental illness. And I didn't know that meditation could initiate a crisis like that.

I wrote the next chapter, *Contraindications for Meditation*, to prevent what happened to my friend from happening to you or someone you know.

The remaining chapters in Part One will discuss how to structure a solitary retreat, how to practice retreat with psilocybin, and more. I also discuss potential group events with me online and in person.

There are several important topics I'd like to address first. Experienced meditators are likely to be familiar with them, so these are primarily for beginners.

In some cases, these themes also apply to psychedelics.

There *is* such a thing as too much meditation.

As you'll see later in the chapter *Suggested Progression*, I recommend meditating every day. But for beginners, this can be too much. The risk of forcing yourself to meditate every day even when you don't feel like it is that you may become bored and stop altogether.

Or worse, it could put an unusual amount of pressure on your psyche, which could lead to serious issues related to what is discussed in the chapter *Contraindications for Meditation*.

The best way to progress is to start slowly. **Ignore my recommendation in *Suggested Progression* to practice every day.** Give yourself weeks or even months to get to that point. Even then, know that it's perfectly fine to take time off occasionally. Anyway, nobody's watching, nobody's keeping score.

Releasing perfectionistic tendencies will keep your path organic and propel you with curiosity and inspiration instead of unreasonable expectations or unhealthy self-disciplining.

Time matters as much as the technique, if not more.

Don't be too concerned about finding the "best" technique. In the chapter *Solitary Meditation Retreat Practice*, I explain that you don't do retreat - retreat does *you*. Spending multiple hours alone in a quiet environment has a power of its own regardless of the method you use to work with your mind.

Introduction to this Path

Daily meditation, or at least meditating most days of the week, will benefit you over months and years regardless of what technique you choose.

All techniques are difficult the first few times you try them. But if one remains difficult after giving it a fair shot, it might not be the one for you, so try a different one. An ill-suited technique will prevent you from experiencing its intended benefits.

How well you follow the technique matters less than how much time you allow for it to affect you. Meditating at moderate proficiency with a technique for forty-five minutes will do much more for you over the years than doing it perfectly for only ten.

Much, if not most of your transformation will come from developing a relationship with the technique, not from being perfectionistic.

How you live affects your meditation more than how much meditation affects your life.

Sometimes people approach meditation with the expectation that it will improve their life. But it's more of a chicken-and-the-egg type of problem. If your life is in disarray, it's likely your mind won't be settled enough to have a productive meditation session. As disappointing as it might seem, we must cultivate peace in our daily lives to experience peace during meditation.

If physical, emotional, or other types of violence are a regular occurrence for you regardless of whether you're the perpetrator or victim, it isn't practical to expect your mind to settle enough in forty-five minutes. The exception would be if you completely lack empathy, as in severe personality disorders.

The same applies to how you spend your recreational time, what you watch on TV, and what you do on the internet and social media. It's unreasonable to expect one hour of meditation to undo the overstimulation and psychological damage of watching several hours of digital garbage.

So, consider what you do for a living, how you spend your free time, and the quality of your relationships. If you want to experience peace, love, and understanding during your meditation session, you must cultivate peace, love, and understanding throughout the rest of the day.

Meditation is *not* about stopping your thoughts.

Some beginners come to the practice having previously adopted the belief that you're not supposed to have thoughts during meditation. Maybe they got that idea from Hollywood. But the brain is constantly processing information and much of it comes out as a stream of ideas, feelings, emotions, and sensations, which is natural.

Periods of non-thought are possible, but they are the side-effect of being profoundly relaxed and shifting one's point of perception to a deeper aspect of consciousness. To put it poetically, we must shift our attention to the depths of the ocean, far beneath the noise of the waves.

The techniques taught in the *Path*[14] do not require you to stop your thoughts or have a thought-free experience. The initial practices teach you how to regard those thoughts. The latter practices teach you how to look deeply into their existential nature. These practices help one develop a productive relationship with the mind and understand one's overall experience of being.

Meditation is *not necessarily* about feeling good.

There's nothing wrong with using meditation for stress reduction or to improve one's mood. It can certainly do that,

---

[14] From this point, "*Path*" will be used as a shortening of the *Path of the Golden Teacher* online program.

and it's better than using unhealthy coping behaviors or substances.

But meditation, at least the way it's taught in the *Path*, goes deeper than that. All feelings are welcome, and you don't need to be in a positive state of mind to engage in the practices. Therefore, don't require yourself to feel "right" to sit down and meditate, because those times are rare. Whatever you feel on a given day, whatever your mood, bring it to your session.

Learning how to weather a storm doesn't happen by stopping the storm, or only training when the sun is out and everything's calm. Learning to weather a storm requires being battered by the wind, stung by the hail, and feeling the chill.

At the end of a session, you might not necessarily feel "good," but you will have made progress in learning how to relate to the various thoughts, emotions, and sensations that arise in daily life. Over time, this can produce a profound level of contentment, the shelter in the storm.

But if your goal is to just feel better, relax, or unload extra stress, there are easier and quicker ways to do that such as massage therapy, walking in nature, exercising, playing games, doing art, playing an instrument, and hanging out with supportive friends and family.

Don't use meditation to avoid your responsibilities.

Be wary if you notice yourself meditating longer than usual, or multiple times per day. You may, unknowingly or not, be using it to avoid your responsibilities. A meditator can slip into placing meditation atop their normal priorities in the name of spirituality.

But as many practitioners in various traditions have concluded, ordinary life is just as sacred as the transcendent. Yet it can become a habit to pay more attention to your breath than to filing your taxes, cleaning your home, finishing homework, or seeing your doctor when needed.

You might develop a special identity as a yogi and behave artificially to match the image. Acting "detached" from everything is a way to hide from, ignore, or bury feelings of hurt, sadness, or other forms of vulnerability.

It's also a terrible justification for neglecting, disrespecting, abandoning, or otherwise abusing other people.

Those familiar with the term *spiritual bypassing* will recognize these warnings.

The same concept applies to someone who uses journeying the same way a spiritual bypasser uses meditation. They might also overuse psychedelics because they regard the hallucinatory state as "more real" than ordinary consciousness. We can label this behavior *psychedelic bypassing*.

Meditation doesn't necessarily make you a better person.

I had been meditating for a decade and a half before one of my spiritual teachers told me to see a therapist. He observed tendencies and behaviors in me that he realized meditation just wasn't going to change. I begrudgingly attended my first therapy session but quickly realized how effective it was and eagerly came back for more.

It is a testament to therapy's potential to heal and change one's behavior that I eventually became a clinical mental health counselor. I recognized the limits of meditation and its teachers and began studying modern psychology.

Today's counseling is based on many decades of scientific observation of mind, behavior, and the efficacy of therapeutic techniques. This approach differs greatly from a culture's folk psychology passed on via its spiritual tradition. That certain knowledge is ancient doesn't automatically mean it's true, effective, or applicable, especially cross-culturally.

While meditating is a powerful tool for investigating the nature of consciousness and reality, it's not necessarily good at producing behavioral change, at least without being paired with modern psychotherapy.

Introduction to this Path

This is especially true for people with conditions like narcissistic personality disorder, borderline personality disorder, and histrionic personality disorder, or at least these conditions' traits.

Unfortunately, behaviors typical in these disorders such as violating others' personal boundaries are often confused with being spiritual, open, and non-judgmental.

Statements like "I don't like using labels" may sound spiritual but should be regarded as red flags since they may be used to avoid accountability.

I've noticed this during long group retreats. There, a disordered person will find themselves surrounded by highly empathetic people primed for kindness and compassion. Without knowing it, good-hearted meditators become unsuspecting suppliers of attention for the disordered person.

It's also possible for the spiritual leader to have a personality disorder and recruit naive seekers to join the flock so they give him or her the adoration they desire.

These considerations also apply to psychedelics, users of psychedelics, leaders of psychedelic groups, and their communities.

The most obvious evidence that meditation and psychedelics don't magically change people for the better is found in social media forums like Facebook groups where aggressive participants behave just like the close-minded bullies and trolls that are found in any other online forum.

Meditation isn't necessarily *intended* to make you a better person.

It's important to be clear on the purpose or goal of any meditative tradition. Modern meditation is often used to improve psychological health. But ancient traditions' goals were existential, not merely for self-help.

For example, the purpose of meditation in Buddhism (broadly speaking since there are various types of Buddhism) is to analyze how the mind works, cease the repetition of patterns that propagate ignorance, craving, and aversion, put an end to the cycle of rebirth, and achieve inner peace.

In some traditions, it is acknowledged that not everyone is suited for that path due to unfortunate circumstances such as being in poor physical or mental health or other challenging life conditions. Not everyone can do this. *And not everyone should.*

But today, some Buddhist and other meditative traditions have made psychological wellness and social welfare a priority, which is distinct from their original spiritual purpose.

Therefore, be aware of a tradition's or teacher's primary goals to ensure they're in line with yours. What do you want for yourself? To heal a trauma or to understand the fundamental nature of reality? These are very different goals, and you don't need to achieve one to achieve the other. But you must decide what's important for you and find a path that suits your needs.

Depending on your goals and your teacher's qualifications, it may be inappropriate for them to act as your therapist. Meditation is not psychotherapy.

For many, a good option is to engage in their path of meditation while meeting with a therapist separately from that context.

It can be easy for a person to interpret their challenge as being of a spiritual nature. This causes them to ignore the possibility their condition has neurological, psychological, social, environmental, or even dietary causes. In these cases, you can't just meditate the problem away.

For some, meditation should be avoided altogether until after having benefitted from therapy and in some cases, medication, especially if they're in a psychologically destabilized or vulnerable state.

Introduction to this Path

Don't use meditation to justify being taken advantage of.

Many contemplative traditions stress the importance of kindness, compassion, patience, and generosity. This is especially alluring to highly empathetic people.

If you are a naturally giving person, and especially if you identify yourself as a people-pleaser, take care not to use your kindness to allow others to take advantage of you.

When wrong is being done, it is time to act, not to regard it as a spiritual test. This is especially pertinent to traditions where followers are told to view their teacher as some type of perfect being, and that no matter how they treat you, it's for your own good. It's not. It's gaslighting. It's manipulation. It's control.

"Judging" is not the same as using discernment.

On social media and in certain groups, one will observe a proscription against "judging" or being judgmental. This is adopted as a kind of spiritual attitude.

However, I've witnessed people abandoning their discernment because they're fearful of being judgy, therefore mistrusting themselves. This causes them to surrender their healthy boundaries and allow harmful or unhelpful behavior to occur.

Yes, it's important to consider other people's perspectives and guard against one's unhelpful biases. In this way, it can be good to not be too judgy.

But this differs from using common sense and identifying situations and behaviors for what they truly are.

Sometimes the most spiritual or psychologically healthy response is to say "No, I don't accept that behavior. It crosses my boundaries. It's hurtful. It's not okay. I do not agree."

Don't abandon your meditation technique to recreate a peak experience.

You can have a spontaneous mystical experience, become enveloped in bliss, or feel profound peace during a session. And there's certainly nothing wrong with that. These are good indications of meditative development.

However, be careful not to chase the experience in future sessions. If you try to recreate it, you might accidentally abandon the technique you were following when the peak experience occurred. Instead, you'll do other things with your mind such as reviving the memory of the experience (but not the experience itself) to try to get it back.

If you'd like to have a similar event again, be faithful to the meditation technique that prompted it, not the experience itself. Don't forget the common instruction to "let go," which includes releasing your desire to re-experience the event.

Ironically, the craving for the experience could be the very thing that blocks it from ever occurring again.

And there are other reasons you may never have the experience again or have it in quite the same way even if you do an excellent job of letting go and following the instructions.

This conundrum shows us that we are never in complete control of our mental events or our lives. It teaches us acceptance and that the individual is part of a larger whole, not independent of it.

Dream journaling helps with meditation.

With practice, we become more sensitive to subtle mental events, the ones we normally don't notice when going about our day. An easy way to develop that sensitivity is to improve your dream recollection. Normal, healthy sleep includes periods of REM (random eye movement). The longest REM periods occur in the final sleep cycles before

Introduction to this Path

waking up, which is why our early morning dreams are the longest and most vivid.

If you don't remember dreaming, it doesn't mean you didn't dream. It just means your recollection isn't well-developed. And the easiest way to improve your recollection is by keeping a dream journal.

By setting the intention to remember your dreams, and by setting a journal and pen on your nightstand, you'll begin to remember last night's glimmers. Write them down as soon as you wake up, even if you only have a few words.

Day by day, week by week, you'll remember even more of the previous night's events. Eventually, you might find yourself recording two or three dreams at a time. You'll notice your capacity to observe subtle mental events during meditation improving too, which in our context is the whole point of practicing dream recollection.

Experiencing "the ultimate" doesn't release you from following social norms.

Whether using meditation, psychedelics, or both, it's possible to have a peak experience. Your peak experience will probably be shaped by your spiritual ideals, philosophy, and belief system. Peak experiences have been described as:

- achieving unity consciousness
- "Seeing that God is me and I am God."
- ego death
- knowing that everything is perfect just as it is
- Nirvana
- Heaven on earth
- experiencing apotheosis, divinization, or enlightenment

These are temporary experiences, but there is the risk of becoming attached to them and feigning their endurance, pretending to be in that state even though it has already faded away.

This is especially risky if the experience causes the person's identity to become inflated. Publicly proclaiming themselves creates a need to constantly reinforce their identity even after the experience has evaporated.

There is a more significant concern, however. Having glimpsed reality from a perspective where ordinary rules of existence no longer apply, it's possible to believe that they shouldn't apply in daily life.

Acting as if "everything is perfect" or "nothing really matters anyway" can have harmful effects even if it's ultimately true. These attitudes can cause us to disregard social norms and boundaries to our own and others' detriment.

The most obvious examples of this are seen in the reports of abusive cult leaders. But you don't have to be a cult leader to abandon your sense of social responsibility and hurt those around you because you think you're "awake."

I imagine that a truly evolved person would understand that even though they are "awake," the people around them probably aren't, or at least don't feel like they are. Those people still rely on that person to behave respectfully, reliably, and to fulfill their responsibilities as regular members of society.

Why the word "ego" isn't used here.

The word "ego" is problematic because its definition varies depending on who's using it.

From a Freudian perspective, the ego is only one of three distinct parts of one's personality. There is the *id*, concerned with unconscious sexual and aggressive drives. There is also the *superego*, concerned with morality. The *ego*'s role is to balance the id and superego.

However, some spiritual practitioners usually equate the ego to the sense of self and regard it as a pathological

Introduction to this Path

issue. To them, the ego is something to be minimized or destroyed for spiritual achievement. This attitude lacks sophistication, though.

For us to operate in the world, and to be human, requires a personality, boundaries, and drive. Peak experiences can temporarily dissolve one's separateness from the rest of reality, but that state is unsustainable.

We can't remain frozen on our meditation cushions until the day we die. And we can't lie on the couch forever after smoking a breakthrough dose of DMT. Eventually, we must get up, go to work, laugh, cry, be with others, grow, and experience life.

Without our personalities or the ability to differentiate the "me" from "you," we can't experience life.

Misunderstanding the role of ego can lead a person into depression and anxiety because they believe it's bad to have an identity, to be themselves. Also, problematic teachers take advantage of this "egoless" view as an excuse to insult, belittle, and gaslight their students.

We should strive to have healthy egos. A healthy sense of self can keep one grounded enough to have peak experiences without losing touch with everyday life. A healthy ego allows a person to grow in a way that promotes well-being, healthy relationships, and an appreciation for simply being human.

When you read books discussing how the ego should be regarded on the spiritual path, it's important to learn what the author's specific definition of ego is. It might not be the same as yours.

To avoid confusion, the word ego won't be used after this chapter. More specific terminology is used to make the point.

Why the word "enlightenment" isn't used here.

Like "ego," the word "enlightenment" means something different depending on who you talk to. For a Christian, enlightenment can mean the entrance into heaven upon death. Or it could mean experiencing heaven on Earth while still alive. If you ask several Christians to write down their personal definition of enlightenment, they're likely to differ at least to some degree.

The same thing goes for Buddhism. If you ask a Theravadan monk, Vajrayana (tantric) yogi, and a Zen priest to describe enlightenment to you, you'll get three different responses.

I've even heard people describe their "awakening" as a direct result of watching YouTube videos. Others said they awakened after having a near-death experience or seeing a UFO.

The point is enlightenment and awakening mean different things to different people.

These words can be problematic because they frame the purpose of spirituality as the attainment of a particular state. This causes seekers to ignore their present life and focus on an imagined future. No matter how much their meditation instructions say to remain in the present, beneath the surface their psyche longs for something different.

A sure way to remain unhappy, depressed, and anxious is to constantly believe true happiness is somewhere else, sometime in the future, after conquering one's sense of self.

The great potential for psychedelics and the meditation instructions of many of the world's traditions is to help us realize that we are already enough just as we are, right here, right now.

Introduction to this Path

You can't obtain wisdom by reading.

Spiritual transformation occurs in a person when they have a significant *experience*. Experience is not the same as reading about a philosophy, technique, or its result. It's not about watching videos or listening to podcasts about spirituality, which only provide information – concepts without experience.

If you want to change your experience of being alive, you will need to practice the meditations for a significant period. It's not an overnight process. It doesn't matter whether you do the *Path of the Golden Teacher* online program[15] or use another system of practice. But do something, do it regularly, and do it long enough to reap the benefits.

If you have one free hour in your day, it's more important to spend it practicing your preferred technique instead of reading a book or listening to a podcast about it.

The same could be said about reading about psychedelic experiences versus having one yourself. Don't be surprised if, after your first journey, you lose interest in reading books about other's experiences or the latest research.

Nothing compares to the real thing.

---

[15] The techniques in the online program are accompanied by commentary and teachings not included in this book.

CONTRAINDICATIONS FOR MEDITATION

The following are reasons to not practice intensive meditation or to meditate only with the close personal supervision of an experienced instructor. You will notice some of these are also listed in the contraindications for psychedelics in Part Two.

Being under the age of 25

People are particularly at risk of developing psychosis or other mental health conditions between the ages of 18 and 25, and intensive meditation can trigger mental illness.

For extra safety and the assurance of maturity, I recommend people be at least 30 years old before engaging the *Path's* online guided meditation program.

30-year-olds are distant from the high-risk age range and more likely to possess the patience, resiliency, and self-efficacy necessary to properly engage the *Path*.

Contraindications for Meditation

And by that age, their life has probably given them sufficient incentive to engage in self-inquiry, spiritual exploration, and mental self-care.

Bipolar disorder, schizophrenia, dissociative conditions, or a history of experiencing psychotic breaks

Meditation can increase the risk of triggering or activating any of these in someone with a pre-existing condition. Remember that in a sense, meditation is a planned and temporary departure from the everyday state of awareness and ordinary reality, which *can* be safe for those without mental health risks, symptoms, or conditions.

Severe pain or injury in the back, neck, hips, or shoulders

Sitting still for extended periods can exacerbate painful or debilitating physical conditions. Meditators with these conditions should choose a posture that causes as little discomfort as possible, even if it means lying down and using supports like pillows or bolsters. They should also shorten their meditation periods to avoid worsening their symptoms.

Feeling significant pain throughout a meditation session prevents one from fruitfully engaging the instructions and experiencing the intended psycho-physical effect.

Insomnia or other sleep-related disturbances and disorders

Meditation can have the effect of heightening one's focus and alertness resulting in hypervigilance. This is especially possible for those with PTSD.[16] Subsequently, one may have trouble falling and remaining asleep.

---

[16] https://en.wikipedia.org/wiki/Hypervigilance

Even those for whom sleep is not a problem may begin to experience difficulties after meditating at night.

For anybody who has trouble with sleep, I recommend meditating in the morning rather than later in the day or right before going to bed.

Suicidal ideation or previous suicide attempts

Meditation can amplify emotions and thought patterns, especially in beginners. Therefore, if you are prone to the following:

- rumination
- existential crisis
- loss of meaning
- feeling directionless
- loneliness
- depression
- helplessness
- profound and unacknowledged anger about harm or injustice that has been inflicted on you
- a persistent desire to punish someone or make them acknowledge how they harmed you - but are powerless to do so

… then it's possible for those or other suicide-related thoughts and emotions to arise during or after meditation.

Suicide is complicated and often occurs without warning. Therefore, it's possible to be at risk for suicide even without meeting the criteria listed here.

Contraindications for Meditation

SUICIDE HOTLINE

If you're in the United States and are having thoughts of suicide, please **call or text 988** for help or visit **https://988lifeline.org**.

If you're outside the U.S., please look up your local suicide prevention services and make sure you know how to access them should you disregard the contraindication and engage in daily meditation, a weekend intensive, or longer retreats.

MEDITATION AS A PROTECTIVE MEASURE

The coming chapter *Suggested Progression* describes the meditation techniques taught in the online program *Path of the Golden Teacher*, for which this book was primarily written. They are designed to prepare the mind to have a powerful and revelatory spiritual experience with the help of a psychedelic.

However, those techniques and meditation in general also serve to prepare the mind for undergoing a psychedelic experience regardless of the intention for the journey. This means that if you have been meditating regularly for a significant period, regardless of the tradition, technique, or system, you may automatically benefit from all that training when the time comes for your journey.

Your meditation history can serve as a protective factor, supporting your ability to cope with what is essentially an extreme state of mind temporarily disconnected from everyday reality while experiencing non-ordinary perception.

Meditation as a Protective Measure

If you have not consistently practiced meditation before, then the *Path of the Golden Teacher* might be your first step. But it doesn't have to be. It's not your only option and it's not necessarily the best option for you.

There are countless teachers, groups, and online programs for you to choose from.[17] They can all benefit you to one degree or another, so it's just a matter of choosing one and dedicating your time and energy to applying their technique(s) regularly.

It's important for you to differentiate between truly transformative meditation from brief techniques for short-term stress reduction or to "feel better." Thanks to neuroplasticity, our brains physically change in response to internal and external experiences. And because of neuroplasticity, the right kind of meditation will stimulate long-term changes in the brain.

But it takes time and the steady application of positive stress. This means a regular practice, daily, if possible, of sessions lasting a significant period.

Occasionally using a meditation app to listen to a five- or ten-minute guided meditation won't stimulate neurological development the way a substantial practice will.

The following pages explain how long-term meditation practice can support you during your psychedelic journey.

---

[17] Some of the videos in the online program are **free** to watch. I also have a **totally free** mini-course titled *Guided Meditation Journeys* I released several years ago. My *Vagus Nerve Stimulation* course may also be helpful. You can find them www.LifeTending.net/OnlineCourses.html.

Enhanced capacity to remain calm and stable regardless of mental and physical arisings.

Many techniques include the instruction to observe thoughts, emotions, and bodily sensations as they arise, but to not react to them. Long-term practice helps a person become much less reactive to these events than usual and remain a neutral observer instead.

A journeyer will experience a myriad of thoughts and emotions over several hours. Some of these may be sad, infuriating, or cause remorse among others. Aside from nausea, the journeyer may also experience headache and flu-like symptoms like muscle aches, shivering, and feeling too cold or warm.

If the person can remain as neutral as possible while experiencing them, this will help prevent or reduce the onset of fear, anxiety, or displeasure.

Enhanced capacity to be attentive for extended periods.

One aspect of meditation is to continually observe an object of attention such as the breath, a part of the body, a verbal phrase, a visualized image, or a physical object in the room. When one's attention is broken, the meditator can recognize the distraction and redirect their mind to the intended object.

Distraction isn't a problem or a failure. It's a valuable opportunity for growth.

Generally, psychedelic journeys are so intriguing that becoming distracted isn't an issue. Still, it's possible to space out during a journey.

Although the visuals can be obvious behind the blindfold, it's possible to miss or ignore subtle insights and emotions as they emerge from one's subconscious mind.

Spending months and years learning how to pay consistent attention to subtle impressions for long periods will help

Meditation as a Protective Measure

ensure you don't miss subtle yet still valuable occurrences during a journey.

Increased openness to and acceptance of one's emotions.

Before learning how to meditate, a person may tend to ignore or suppress certain emotions. This can happen for a variety of reasons such as being raised in a family, culture, or religion where certain emotions are off-limits. Or someone raised by or in a relationship with a narcissist might have learned to keep certain feelings to themselves for self-preservation.

Meditating can help that person acknowledge their unexpressed feelings, stop the automatic tendency to suppress them, accept them, and eventually gain the skill and courage to communicate them to others in a constructive fashion.

As mentioned before, various emotions can arise during a journey, including those ordinarily labeled negative and those which are typically ignored. Since meditation trains one to open up to new feelings without being reactive, this can help one accept these feelings during a journey. This is especially important because those feelings will be greatly amplified due to the psychedelic effect.

Increased openness to and acceptance of strange thoughts and sensations.

Just like suppressed emotions, strange thoughts and sensations can arise in meditation. Hearing voices and odd sounds, seeing unusual lights, losing sensation in parts of the body, feeling completely disconnected from one's body, and feeling as if spinning inside one's body are examples of what can occur especially during long periods of meditation.

The instruction is to observe these events with neutrality while noticing their temporary nature. Everything passes in time.

Similar thoughts and sensations can occur during the psychedelic journey and be far more pronounced. Previous training in staying cool and collected while these things happen will be important at that time.

Enhanced capacity to delay gratification.

Meditation can help a person decompress from a hectic day or cope with behavioral triggers. But it can still take a half-hour or longer to begin to feel those effects. Profound psychological change and the receipt of spiritual insight can require years of practice. This is all to say that meditation is a perfect system for learning delayed gratification.[18]

The willingness to invest time and energy long before achieving one's reward is a sign of maturity. It develops one's patience, which is an invaluable asset for personal relationships, higher education, and one's career.

The psychedelic journey is not a silver bullet. Although it can make tremendous headway in healing trauma, it often needs to be paired with a period of therapy or counseling for sustained change. Those hoping for immediate healing and resolution may be disappointed to learn it takes time.

Therefore, the maturity one gains from slowly and patiently cultivating the benefits of meditation will help set reasonable expectations for their journey.

Enhanced capacity for self-inquiry.

Meditation's inward focus naturally increases one's capacity for investigating psychological patterns, biases, hopes, fears, and what makes them tick. Understanding why one does what one does and says what one says in response to a situation can increase one's sense of freedom and wisdom.

---

[18] For more on delayed gratification, I recommend the book *The Marshmallow Test: Why Self-Control is the Engine of Success* by Walter Mischel.

Meditation as a Protective Measure

Instead of always responding the same way, the person can identify a habitual response before they act on it and choose a different course instead.

Looking inward also develops one's sense of meaning. Meaning is crucial for psychological health and happiness. If you know why you are the way you are, you'll have confidence in being that person and believe that you have every right to exist and thrive in this world.

But if you'd rather not see who you are deep inside or why you are the way you are, it's better not to take a psychedelic journey. It's possible for your unconscious drives, hopes, and fears to be thrust into the limelight, impossible to ignore.

Enhanced resiliency and emotional self-management.

Resilient people know how to cheer themselves up when they feel down. They're able to weather periodic emotional storms without drowning. They understand that if they hang on long enough, things will get better and that having a good attitude is half the battle.

Meditation cultivates these qualities. When starting a session, the meditator cannot predict exactly what thoughts, emotions, memories, fantasies, or anxieties will arise before it's over. Their main task is to notice when these things arise without blocking or altering them. They must allow the event to come and go at its own pace.

Eventually, the meditator realizes that every thought and emotion is temporary. "Everything passes" is cliché. But many spiritual phrases are cliché only until they become a lived experience.

Only when a person realizes the truth that "everything passes" in their bones does their experience of being alive significantly change.

When a journeyer experiences a challenging trip, simply reminding them, "Hang on! Your journey will be over soon, anyway" can be effective in calming them down.

A journeyer with a long history of meditation already knows how to "hang on" because they do it every time they practice. The don't hang on to anything, though. They endure.

Also, there exist techniques designed to promote a sense of well-being and happiness during a session, for example, the practice of loving-kindness, included in this path and in various Buddhist lineages.

These types of practices teach the meditator they can do a lot to improve their mood without waiting for external circumstances to do it for them.

This level of self-management helps during a psychedelic journey because it's possible for the journey to take a sad or frightening turn at some point.

If the journeyer is an experienced meditator, they'll be able to apply their training and shift their mood toward the positive using intention, visualization, or other spiritual resources like prayer when things take a downturn.

As you'll read in Part Two, changing the playlist or taking off one's blindfold during a challenging journey are also good self-management techniques.

Flexible sense of self.

One's sense of self is a combination of memories, expectations, beliefs, preferences, dislikes, physical body, and more. Life is the continuous arising and passing of experiences. And our body is the constant birth and death of tissue cells. The self, then, is the integrating of life experiences with one's body and mind. For people with spiritual worldviews, one's spirit, soul, or non-physical consciousness, etc., is also integrated into the self.

Essentially, the self isn't a thing, it's a process. It's a temporary conglomeration of multiple ever-changing factors.

Nevertheless, a healthy sense of self is relatively constant over time, and most changes are imperceptible. One's personality operates within a reliable set of upper and

Meditation as a Protective Measure

lower limits, with a predictable set of behaviors. Major deviations in the self are rare and can be due to unexpected causes such as trauma, illness, or the loss of a loved one.

They can also occur at expected points of the human growth and development cycle such as puberty, leaving home, pregnancy, giving birth, parenting, and developing one's professional identity.

There are many other ways in which a person's sense of self can change slowly or quickly.

Long-term meditators become intimately familiar with the moment-by-moment changes occurring in their minds and bodies through simple, focused observation.

Some meditators learn to observe typically ignored states like sleep and dreaming. During these times, one's selfhood is remarkably different from when one is awake, but non-meditators don't notice it as much.

Either by textual study or through natural observation, meditators become keenly aware of their mortality. By carefully observing bodily and mental changes (aging), death's inevitability becomes a conscious fact.

Being dead may not bother people because, after all, they won't be able to feel it. But the act of dying is another matter altogether. Fortunately, it's possible to prepare for dying by paying attention when falling asleep and dreaming.

As difficult as it may be, staying conscious during these transitions can remove the fear of the unknown and the fear of extreme changes to one's sense of self.

Meditation develops the degree of sensitivity and stability necessary to stay conscious long enough to perceive these transitions as they occur.

Because of this, long-term meditators are more accustomed to experiencing subtle and drastic changes in their sense of self, which can make those changes more tolerable. They can even develop positive curiosity about these transitions, including their approaching death.

The psychedelic journey is an extreme shift in the sense of self and for that reason alone can be highly distressing for the person. One's senses can be confused whereby sights are heard and sounds are seen (synesthesia). The body can feel drastically different.

Unexpected memories can arise, including negative or hurtful events. Or one can be overcome by new inspirations and concepts which, even though carry a positive tone, are still overwhelming. There can be a sudden urge to change one's behavior, lifestyle, or relationships.

Depending on one's belief system, entering the psychedelic state can be analogous to the act of dying. After lying down, the journeyer's perception of this reality fades away, sometimes accompanied by physical discomfort, and is replaced by otherworldly scenes and visitations from non-human beings or deceased people.

Since meditators are more attuned to the reality that selfhood is a process, not a solid, singular constant, the psychedelic experience will be like advanced training for realizing that perspective as a felt experience.

They can also regard the psychedelic journey as advanced preparation for the moment of death. Aside from experiencing an extreme identity shift, it's possible to receive visual or noetic insights regarding one's participation in the selfhood of the universe itself.

The journeyer has an opportunity to realize (again, as a felt experience) their interconnectedness with everything else, and see their brief existence (birth, growth, death) as a natural aspect of life. This can reduce or eliminate the journeyer's fear of eventual dissolution by coming to peace about how things truly are, including that the whole universe experiences a birth, growth, and dissolution of its own.

Meditation as a Protective Measure

Capacity to remain in a state of "not knowing."

Every psychedelic journey is unique. And for first-timers, it's a mystery. Much of what occurs is beyond description, so they can't be well oriented ahead of time. And the hallucinations are only a portion of what occurs over several hours.

In meditation, the practitioner trains in *not knowing*. This occurs naturally since meditation involves moment-by-moment observation of what comes next, and there's no way for the beginner to reliably predict the emotions, thoughts, and memories that will arise during an entire session.

Therefore, if the journeyer has previous meditation training, this will help them stay calm and grounded as unpredictable experiences arise during the journey. It also helps with daily life.

As a side note, meditation also trains people to be in a state of not knowing by placing them in a situation where they will not reflexively access their mobile device for a specific period. How often do we check our phones while standing in line, riding the elevator, driving, watching TV, or even during conversation?

Aside from entertainment, we're checking our inboxes and messaging services to make sure we know our status in life. When we check our phones, we wonder if there's an emergency to deal with, if there's a work opportunity, if someone is thinking about us, or if there are other situations we believe we need to be aware of at that moment to be comfortable. That comfort comes from knowing our place in the world.

But we don't need to constantly check our digital status to be happy. In fact, the constant confirmation-seeking only causes more stress and insecurity.

What we need to be truly happy is to know our status in our actual lives. This means having a clear awareness of our physical bodies as well as our genuine emotions and thoughts.

Not those that were produced by looking at a phone or laptop, but the ones that originate from within, without external conditioning from electronics.

Meditation requires us to silence our devices and set them aside. For many people, an hour of meditation may be the longest, or only, period of their day when they do not check their phones. This may be exactly why some people constantly feel anxious. Too much screen time.

The beginner may feel compelled to interrupt their meditation to glance at their device. Those moments are opportunities to notice the unconscious habit and train in allowing the urge to dissolve without picking up the phone.

With practice, the meditator will realize that true relief comes from freeing oneself from the constant urge to check the device, and not from maintaining their hypervigilance.

Capacity to "know."

For experienced meditators, mental events become somewhat predictable. Whether in a formal session or over the normal course of the day, we observe how one thought leads to the next based on pre-existing patterns, preferences, and aversions. There are no truly random thoughts.

We realize that when we remember a certain person or event, the memory kicks off a well-rehearsed mental script. We see that our responses to traffic, coworkers, and other situations don't change much on a day-to-day basis. In a life experienced without awareness, there are no original thoughts, only constant replay.

But the power of observation and the patience we develop in meditation grants us the choice to respond to life's situations differently. We can also choose not to respond at and simply notice, witness, and let go instead.

Through meditation training, we can rewrite our daily script and engage in our lives differently, leading toward greater happiness. We already know the thoughts and actions

Meditation as a Protective Measure

that don't work for us because we've repeated them countless times. Why not take a chance and try something different?

Noticing one's train of thought and changing its course is directly applicable to the psychedelic journey. With proper meditation training, the journeyer will notice the early indicators of a downward spiral.

Meditation makes it easier to encourage positive states of mind from within instead of relying on external stimuli.

Rather than surrendering to the trip's negative trajectory, the journeyer can use their meditation training to change their thought pattern, shifting it in a positive direction.

It can be as simple as acknowledging the need to change course, sitting up, removing one's blindfold for a couple of minutes, changing the playlist to something happier, then re-entering the journey.

It can happen more directly by applying a mood-changing meditation technique like the ones practiced in the Heart series of the online program.

The bravest journeyers may opt to experience their challenging trip without changing it at all. They exemplify total acceptance and the courage necessary to be open to thoughts and feelings other people would normally flee from.

INTEGRATION MEDITATION

There is a type of meditation that can occur spontaneously as well as intentionally, which I'll refer to as *integration meditation*. While integration usually applies to the period following a psychedelic journey, in this case, it refers to the general integration of thoughts and emotions about life during one's daily meditation practice.

It occurs *spontaneously* when one is trying to use a specific technique but is having trouble staying on task. In this case, the meditator may feel inept or lazy because of their inability to effectively apply the technique during that session. Instead, they're highly distracted, daydreaming, or ruminating for most if not all of the session.

It's a common occurrence for a meditator to sit down intending to apply a specific technique then hear their alarm mark the end of the session and realize they had been lost in thought the entire time. This realization is often paired with disappointment.

However, the disappointment is misplaced. Our brains are constantly digesting thoughts about the past, present, and

Integration Meditation

future to help us adapt to our environment, survive, and thrive. When we sit down to meditate and find ourselves distracted, it can sometimes be because we have front-row seats to our internal mental processes and our brain is particularly focused on a specific topic at that time.

If during meditation you're distracted by thoughts about an important project at work, a recent breakup, financial worry, or a painful life event, understand that it means these thoughts are a higher priority for your brain than, say, relaxing while feeling the sensation of the breath as it enters and leaves your body.

Your thoughts become so loud during meditation because you're finally undistracted and now can do nothing but pay attention to them. Up to the moment you sat down to meditate, you were too busy with work tasks, entertainment, technology, and other people's issues to give your personal concerns the conscious attention they deserve.

Therefore, don't feel bad about the session when you're unable to apply your chosen meditation technique. You've organically shifted into integration meditation instead. Don't be surprised if it takes several integration meditation sessions before your mind is resolved enough about those issues to settle down and follow a specific technique.

In the case of *intentional* integration meditation, you sit in a meditation posture while allowing thoughts and emotions to grab your attention. Instead of remaining disengaged from them the way you normally would when following a technique, you let yourself get involved. Think of it as a form of Gedankenexperiment.

Gedankenexperiment means "thought experiment" in German. Albert Einstein is frequently associated with his Gedankenexperiments. For example, he developed his ideas about relativity by visualizing looking at a clock while riding a beam of light.

Your version of Gedankenexperiment might look like imagining different versions of a conversation, argument, or negotiation you know you'll be having soon. Or you might weigh the pros and cons of choosing one career path over another. Or you might imagine what life will be like after the approaching death of a parent or the finalization of a divorce.

The combination of time and creativity can help your brain resolve these issues. But sitting down for the sake of quiet introspection is a lost art. These days, when most of us sit down or stand in line we immediately hold a flat screen up to our face. We prioritize information originating outside ourselves over information arising from within.

We're barely experiencing our true lives because of this. What a shame it would be if on our deathbeds we realized most of our life was spent passively watching a show.

If you're following the online meditation program, consider inserting integration meditation sessions into your schedule. Not only will it allow you to regularly process your life with conscious awareness, but it'll also make you more available for the sessions when you do use a specific technique.

The instructions for integration meditation are simple. Just sit in meditation posture, let the thoughts come, and let yourself get fully involved in them. If you can, let the session go as long as necessary for the thoughts to lose steam or for you to get bored. Those are signs that your brain has successfully processed its concerns.

At that point, you can either end the session or continue by applying a specific meditation technique.

This technique can also be used for psychedelic integration. It happens naturally, anyway. Instead of sitting in meditation posture, you might spend the afternoon or evening following a journey lying in bed or on the couch letting your mind organically drift while reflecting on the experience.

If you choose to do a solitary retreat that includes a psychedelic journey (described in one of the following chapters), consider including integration meditation in your practice schedule for the day after your journey while you're

Integration Meditation

still in retreat. It may even be something you do for days or weeks afterward.

SOLITARY MEDITATION RETREAT PRACTICE

Solitary retreat is a powerful discipline for transformation and maturing your practice of meditation. It's especially pertinent in these modern times when we are becoming increasingly aware of the debilitating effects of technology addiction and overstimulation.

A solitary retreat has three aspects: being alone, being undistracted, and dedicating most hours of the day to meditation. The remaining time is spent sleeping, eating, exercising, and being in nature.

Framing it neurologically, solitary meditation retreat practice is a strict form of dopamine fasting. Many of us are constantly overstimulated by looking at the internet many hours of the day, and our neurotransmitters are out of balance. Thus, we become addicted to constant stimulation.

Beginners often feel edgy, bored, or distracted when learning how to meditate. The mind can seem like a rushing

Solitary Meditation Retreat Practice

river of thoughts. For the younger meditator, sexual fantasies and the accompanying physical arousal can be a nuisance, especially if they don't understand these are, in a way, withdrawal symptoms.

Sitting quietly and solely paying attention to one's breath or one's body for ten minutes, let alone a whole hour, can seem extremely challenging for them especially if they are addicted to their computers, gaming systems, and mobile devices. But constant distraction is not a modern invention.

For thousands of years, yogis of various traditions have spent days, weeks, months, and years utterly alone in the wild so they could plumb the depths of their minds for spiritual fulfillment.

They sought places of solitude in jungles, forests, and mountain caves far enough from civilization to prevent interruption by other humans.

Many of these yogis prioritized their spiritual mission so highly they prevented the possibilities of getting married, having children, or earning an income. They sacrificed their social identities so they could focus on one thing, meditation.

There were periods in my younger life when I prioritized going on solitary retreats as well as group intensives. I have spent from ten days to a whole month inside small rustic cabins in the mountains of Colorado without human contact, television, the internet, and indoor plumbing so that I could meditate for ten, twelve, or more hours each day without distraction.

At the time, I believed the main benefit of those retreats was the ability to go deeper during meditation, and then being able to access those new depths after returning home to my ordinary schedule.

Now I realize there was another important benefit. These retreats served as dopamine fasts. Each one was like going cold turkey for my addiction to entertainment, noise, distraction, overstimulation, and constant pleasure seeking.

Path of the Golden Teacher

The withdrawals were real. The first couple of days were usually the most challenging because my brain need adjust to the sudden loss of stimulation. I usually had trouble staying awake during the day and staying asleep at night. I also experienced mood swings.

I thought the pronounced anxiety I felt at the start of each retreat was simply from being in a new environment, but now I know that was only part of it. My brain was readjusting because I had put myself in a peaceful environment, and it was uncomfortable.

But when the adjustment was complete, I was able to meditate better because my mind no longer had to compete with the digital world for my attention. Instead of being boring, true peacefulness had become interesting and worthwhile.

And instead of darting in every direction like cockroaches when the lights came on, my mind felt steady, strong, and focused.

I also remembered how important the people in my life were to me. Being in solitary retreat caused me to miss them dearly. It was partly out of loneliness, sure. But it was also because, like my own mind, my memory of them no longer had to compete with the digital world.

By being undistracted, I realized how much I loved them and how much I had taken them for granted.

Solitary retreat is not only an excellent way to explore one's mind, but also a powerful way to reignite one's love of friends, family, our planet, and all the creatures on it.

Solitary retreat is not only an event, but it's a practice unto itself. In a way, it doesn't matter what kind of meditation technique you do in retreat because retreat will work on you in its own way, regardless. I once heard an apt saying, "You don't do retreat. Retreat does *you*." And it's true.

Most meditators using the online program will be typically modern people. You might be in a relationship, have children, and have one or more jobs with limited vacation

Solitary Meditation Retreat Practice

time every year. Spending a week or longer in a secluded cabin may not interest you or may not be feasible even if you are.

But even one day alone wholly dedicated to meditation can have profound effects on your experience of mind. And you don't need to go anywhere, you can create a retreat environment in your own home. All you need is a room where you can be alone all day, without interruption.

The word "environment" implies external conditions, but that's only part of it. The retreat environment is also based on behaviors you commit to for the duration of your retreat.

The following page lists several commitments you can make. You must consider each one in the context of your life and use it only if it makes practical sense.

Commitments to help create a retreat environment at home:

- I will maintain silence for the duration of my retreat, not speaking to anyone in my home or over the phone. (If you live with someone, you should ask for their support ahead of time. They should understand that they are not to communicate with you in any way unless there's an emergency.)

- I will not read any books, magazines, or digital media.

- I will not write notes, text messages, or communicate on social media.

- I will silence my phone and put it out of sight until the retreat is done.

- I will not access my laptop until the retreat is done.

- My main activity for the retreat will be to meditate according to the schedule I create for myself. I will abstain from unrelated activities or entertainment. I will only exercise, rest, and eat, according to schedule.

CAUTION:

If you begin to disconnect from reality (beyond what is usual for meditation), become manic/hyper, deeply depressed, anxious, or frightened, end your retreat immediately, and ground yourself in ordinary activities to let the pressure out. If necessary, contact a mental health professional such as a counselor or therapist.

Solitary Meditation Retreat Practice

The last commitment listed on the previous page implies that you've created a schedule for your retreat. The following pages include sample schedules you might use. Ultimately, you should design a schedule that you are comfortable with and are inspired to adhere to. Your schedule should not be regarded as a challenge, a test, or a measurement of your character. It should only be used as a support structure.

There's no benefit to being extreme or overly challenging, so don't force yourself to meditate beyond your capacity. It's not wise to run a 10K race unless you've run a 5K first, or to run a full marathon without working your way up to that distance over many months. It's the same with meditation.

But being too loose with your schedule can make it easy for you to be distracted and remain in the shallow end of the meditative experience. It's about balance, and that takes time to discover for yourself.

This is no place for perfectionism, though. Kindness and common sense should be your guides.

If it's your first time dedicating a whole day at home to meditation, keep in mind that there will be more opportunities to do it differently in the future. You'll be able to adjust your schedule and your environment next time based on what you learned this time.

If you are using the meditations from the online program, I recommend practicing regularly for three months before doing a one-day solitary retreat. This is an opportunity to deepen your relationship with the techniques you've already been practicing. It's also not the time to learn a brand-new technique.

It can be most fruitful to use only one or two techniques for the whole time (in a one-day retreat) instead of using a different technique for each session. This is a time to go for depth, not breadth.

Sample Schedule for a One-Day At-Home Retreat for *Beginner* Meditators:

Set your alarm to wake up at a time you know will allow you to feel rested. For example, if you normally wake up at 6:00 am during the work week, you might set your alarm for 8:00 am on Saturday and go to bed early the night before to ensure a good night's rest.

The rest of the schedule is based on the example of waking up at 8:00 am, so you'll need to adjust your schedule accordingly. Use an alarm throughout the day to keep yourself on schedule.

8:15 am – 9:00 am:

After waking up and tending to your body's needs, meditate for forty-five minutes.

9:00 am – 10:00 am:

Breakfast, shower (if desired), and a brief walk outside or some light stretching indoors.

10:00 am – 11:00 am:

Meditate for 45 minutes and use the remaining 15 minutes to do some light stretching, take a brief walk, or just get some fresh air outside.

11:00 am – 12:00 pm:

Meditate for 45 minutes and use the remaining 15 minutes as a break before lunch.

Solitary Meditation Retreat Practice

12:00 – 1:30 pm:

Lunch, cleaning, walking outdoors, light stretching/yoga, napping, etc. If you didn't shower in the morning, showering now could be a nice way to refresh yourself for the afternoon.

1:30 pm - 2:30 pm:

Meditation for 45 minutes, 15-minute break

2:30 pm – 3:30 pm:

Meditation for 45 minutes, 15-minute break

3:30 pm – 4:30 pm:

Meditation for 45 minutes, 15-minute break

4:30 pm – 5:30 pm:

Mid-afternoon break. Have a snack, take a walk, etc.

5:30 – 6:30 pm:

Final meditation session and **end of retreat**. Break silence and return to ordinary life. Don't be surprised if your preference is to stay home and engage in low-stimulation activities for the rest of the evening.

Sample Schedule for *Experienced* Meditators:

This schedule **extends** the previous one by adding:

6:30 – 7:30 pm:

Meditation for 45 minutes, 15-minute break

7:30 pm – 8:00 pm:

Dinner (this is only a half-hour break)

8:00 pm – 9:00 pm:

Meditation for 45 minutes, 15-minute break

9:00 pm – 10:00 pm:

Final meditation session and **end of retreat.**

CAUTION:

It is important to use this schedule only after becoming comfortable with the one for beginners on the previous page. I recommend doing several retreats using the lighter schedule before attempting this one.

It is possible to psychologically hurt yourself by pushing too hard during meditation. This usually occurs by scheduling too many sessions, making the sessions too long, or not relaxing enough during the break periods. When people attempt retreat schedules that are inappropriate for them, they put themselves at **risk of dissociation, re-traumatization, and psychosis.** It's rare, but it happens.

SOLITARY RETREATS WITH PSILOCYBIN

One way to experience a psilocybin journey is by sandwiching it between two meditation days. The first day could follow one of the schedules from the previous chapter while allowing time to reflect on your intentions for your journey and making the necessary preparations.

The middle day could begin with a couple of meditation sessions in the morning, before the journey. That afternoon or evening could be a blend of rest and relaxation, with only a little bit of meditation. It's best to avoid any sense of pressure. Go easy on yourself.

The third day could be dedicated to integration combined with meditation. Include journaling, artwork, music, extended walks in nature, and long naps.

But forgo restrictions on talking to allow for the presence of a sitter during your journey and for making phone calls to supportive friends whenever necessary.

CAUTION:

This type of retreat should only be done by those who have already had several psychedelic journeys on their own and have done several solitary meditation retreats without psychedelics.

GROUP EVENTS WITH THE AUTHOR

It's natural to want to be able to ask questions about the techniques or your progress. You might also want to share your experiences with other meditators using the online program. Therefore, I've created several ways for us to connect:

Group meetings over Zoom

I will use the email address you use to register for the online program to invite you to periodic group meetings over Zoom.

The first invitation will come after you have completed the Foundation series and been enrolled in the program for at least two and a half months. This is to ensure that you have invested sufficient time and answered as many questions as possible on your own by engaging in the practices.

Group Events with the Author

Private Facebook Group

Your first invitation to a Zoom meeting will also include an invitation to a private and hidden Facebook group. The group is intended to help you meet other practitioners, share experiences, and be supportive of each other. There are rules posted on the group's Facebook page which everyone must follow to keep the conversations positive, productive, and pertinent.

The continuing existence of the group will be dependent on how Meta/Facebook's rules and technology evolve and how well group members engage in it.

Group Retreats

Depending on the level of interest expressed by users of the online program, I may periodically offer multi-day retreats in the mountains of Colorado.

These will be opportunities to be without the distraction of everyday life and explore the meditation techniques far more deeply than possible at home.

And while the Zoom meetings and Facebook group are nice ways to connect with others, there's nothing better than meeting fellow practitioners in person.

Whether these retreats will include the use of psilocybin will be determined in time, depending on various factors.

SUPPORT FOR CHALLENGING MEDITATION EXPERIENCES

The following websites offer support, guidance, and information about psychological difficulties during and after daily meditation or intensive retreats:

www.CheetahHouse.org

I recommend listening to interviews with the founder of Cheetah House, Willoughby Britton Ph.D. to become familiar with the risks and potential adverse experiences of meditation. A simple search for her name on YouTube will yield numerous opportunities to listen to her.

I also recommend an interview on the YouTube channel *Guru Viking* with Steve James featuring Dr. Nicholas Van Dam and Chelsey Fasano. The interview is titled *Mind the Hype* and takes a critical look at contemporary mindfulness research.

SUGGESTED PROGRESSION

For readers who intend to use a psychedelic journey as part of this meditation path, it is recommended to accomplish the first thirty-two meditation techniques at the very least before doing so. This means training daily for nine months.

Ideally, readers will complete the first forty-seven meditations before their first (or next) psychedelic journey. At minimum, this will take seventy-four weeks, just over a year and a half.

As I will mention again in Part Two[19], I'm aware of the possibility that a reader may have a terminal illness. In that case, waiting nine months, let alone a year-and-a-half to take their journey may be impossible.

This is the primary reason why I haven't set up an automated schedule restriction for the first thirty-eight meditations in the online program. If you so desire, you can do each meditation as much or as little as you want to before progressing to the next one. You can even skip certain

---

[19] See the chapter *Preparation* in Part Two.

meditations altogether to access the ones that interest you the most.

But I don't recommend that for readers who are not diagnosed with a terminal illness because each guided meditation contains instructions that are meant to be included in the next. So, if you skip a meditation, it's likely that you'll miss out on an important instruction, which could have deleterious effects on your experience with the remaining practices.

I also don't recommend doing a meditation just one time to quickly move through the series. The recommended minimum sessions for some of the meditations is seven, which is one week if you practice daily. Many techniques have a minimum suggested time of several weeks.

However, doing any meditation a certain number of times is not a measure of how much you've changed as a person. Everyone is unique. One person may have a life-changing insight after doing a technique ten times, while another may need to practice it for several months before noticing a subtle change in their thinking pattern. This is one of the reasons this program doesn't offer any type of certificate of completion.

The only marker that truly matters is the beneficial shift in your relationship with yourself and the world around you. One measure of a person who has matured through the practice is they have no desire to brag, announce, or show off about their meditative experiences.

There **is** an automated schedule restriction for the remaining meditations. These include the Nature of Mind series, the Visionary series, the Sleep and Dream series, the Meditation on the External Elements series, and Union Practice/Sexual Yoga.

The schedule is set to give the meditator access to those final series fifty-six weeks after beginning the online program. There are two major reasons for this restriction.

Suggested Progression

The most important reason is that it is unlikely for the meditator to have the intended experience without a very strong foundation in the first thirty-eight practices.

Doing each of them only once is unlikely to yield the type of sensitivity, skill, and maturity required to properly engage the remaining practices. Indeed, even the minimum suggested duration may not be long enough for some if not most meditators using the program. Remember, this path can take a lifetime, and there are no guarantees.

The second reason is administrative. Over-eager readers may register for the online program specifically to access the instructions for the Visionary series and Union Practice/Sexual Yoga, with no interest in training in the preliminary practices.

But if they were to attempt those practices without building a foundation with the first thirty-eight meditations, they would likely have a disappointing, confusing, or frustrating experience.

I understand these practices have a particularly mysterious and titillating aura. This is partly because practices like these are regarded as secret in certain traditions originating in Asia and are restricted to relatively few yogis there. The secrecy only adds to their allure.

There is no fast-forward button for spiritual fulfillment. Anyone who engages in these final practices will quickly realize these are, like the others, still only meditation techniques, and they'll take time.

The meditators who make the most of the first thirty-eight meditations may not even feel the need to accomplish the remaining practices. Or they may not feel any rush to do so.

Everyone who considers registering for the online program should carefully review the cancellation and refund policy before doing so. If you are a mature, patient individual with wholesome intentions for engaging the practices, this won't be an issue.

I recommend using your digital calendar to schedule what time you'll practice meditation each day. It's not necessary to practice at the exact same time each day, though. The point is to set aside *a* time, whatever that time is, each day for meditation.

With the pressure and noise of modern living, it's easy to fill every hour with distraction and entertainment such as internet browsing. So, if you can dedicate an hour per day, and respect your schedule, that will go a long way to having a transformative meditation practice over time.

There is never a perfect time to meditate. It'll never come because it doesn't exist. Understandably, many people seek out meditation as an antidote to a personal challenge like illness, loss of a loved one, or relationship conflict. But the truth is, by then it's too late.

A period of crisis is the most challenging time to learn how to meditate. However, it's the best time to rely on an already-established meditation practice.

So, don't delay. Whether your life is peaceful or chaotic, start now. Book the time in your calendar every day and do it as often as is reasonable, and so long as it does not prevent you from fulfilling your daily responsibilities.

Earlier, I mentioned special considerations for people with terminal illnesses. But we're all terminal, we're all going to die one day, so it's better to prepare now while you have your strength, your wits, and sufficient time still available to you.

The following section will list each meditation and the minimum recommended number of sessions for each. Each description contains a table of cells you can enter a checkmark or a session date for tracking your progress.

Please read each description carefully because they differ. One instruction may say to do the meditation seven days in a row. Another may say to do the meditation only twice or three times but to fill the rest of the week with a prior meditation.

Suggested Progression

Please remember that, especially if you're new to meditation, you should **ignore the instruction to meditate every day**. That can be too much, especially for beginners. Find a pace that works for you, not against you. Meditating three or four days out of the week is a good frequency to start with. But you should still eventually work your way up to a daily practice at a pace appropriate to your personal circumstances.

After you complete the whole program, what you do next is up to you. You might choose to continue meditating regularly while using only the techniques that appeal to you the most. Or you might take a long break and experience the fruits of your work in everyday life. Or you might meditate on an as-needed basis.

You may have begun this program with the intention of including psychedelics, but after a while decided you no longer want to. That's perfectly fine too. It's your decision, and no one knows you better than you know yourself.

The *Path* is only a structure, a tool. It's not meant for you to become dependent on it. When it no longer serves you, let it go.

THE FOUNDATIONAL SERIES

1. Resting attention and softening tension

Recommended *minimum* number of sessions: Seven

> Total duration so far, assuming you meditate *every* day:
> **One week**

Check off each box or write the dates of your sessions inside to help you track your progress.

2. Releasing the weight

Recommended minimum number of sessions: Three. Then go back to meditation #1 and incorporate what you learned from this one. Do four more sessions of #1 this way.

> Total duration so far, assuming you meditate *every* day:
> **Two weeks**

Check off each box or write the dates of your sessions inside to help you track your progress.

Suggested Progression

3. Choosing your battles

Recommended minimum number of sessions: Three. Then go back to meditation #1 and incorporate what you learned from this one as well as #2. Do four more sessions of #1 this way.

> Total duration so far, assuming you meditate *every* day:
> **Three weeks**

Check off each box or write the dates of your sessions inside to help you track your progress.

4. Noticing and releasing tension (lying down)

Recommended minimum number of sessions: Seven.

> Total duration so far, assuming you meditate *every* day:
> **Four weeks**

Check off each box or write the dates of your sessions inside to help you track your progress.

5. Tension release (lying down then sitting up)

Recommended minimum number of sessions: Fourteen. During the sitting-up stage of the practice, incorporate what you learned in #1, #2, and #3.

Total duration so far, assuming you meditate *every* day:
Six weeks

Check off each box or write the dates of your sessions inside to help you track your progress.

6. Absorbing energy (lying down)

Recommended minimum number of sessions: Seven.

Total duration so far, assuming you meditate *every* day:
Seven weeks

Check off each box or write the dates of your sessions inside to help you track your progress.

The Foundational Series

7. Absorbing energy (lying down then sitting up)

Recommended minimum number of sessions: Fourteen. During the sitting-up stage of the practice, incorporate what you learned in #5.

Total duration so far, assuming you meditate *every* day:
Nine weeks

Check off each box or write the dates of your sessions inside to help you track your progress.

8. Smile technique

Recommended minimum number of sessions: One. Then apply the smile technique whenever appropriate and possible through to the end of the Deep Peace series.

THE COGNITIVE SERIES

9. Cognitive Distortion: Filtering

Recommended minimum number of sessions: Two. Then do five more sessions using #1 as the format, incorporating what you learned from this one whenever necessary.

Total duration so far, assuming you meditate *every* day:
Ten weeks

Check off each box or write the dates of your sessions inside to help you track your progress.

10. Cognitive Distortion: Shoulding oneself

Recommended minimum number of sessions: Two. Then do five more sessions using #1 as the format, incorporating what you learned from this one and #9 whenever necessary.

Total duration so far, assuming you meditate *every* day:
Eleven weeks

Check off each box or write the dates of your sessions inside to help you track your progress.

The Cognitive Series

11. Cognitive Distortion: Shoulding others

Recommended minimum number of sessions: Two. Then do five more sessions using #1 as the format, incorporating what you learned from this one and the others from the Cognitive series whenever necessary.

Total duration so far, assuming you meditate *every* day:
Twelve weeks

Check off each box or write the dates of your sessions inside to help you track your progress.

12. Cognitive Distortion: Catastrophizing

Recommended minimum number of sessions: Two. Then do five more sessions using #1 as the format, incorporating what you learned from this one and the others from the Cognitive series whenever necessary.

Total duration so far, assuming you meditate *every* day:
Thirteen weeks

Check off each box or write the dates of your sessions inside to help you track your progress.

13. Cognitive Distortion: Control Fallacy

Recommended minimum number of sessions: Two. Then do five more sessions using #1 as the format, incorporating what you learned from this one and the others from the Cognitive series whenever necessary.

Total duration so far, assuming you meditate *every* day:
Fourteen weeks

Check off each box or write the dates of your sessions inside to help you track your progress.

THE HEART SERIES

14. Gratitude

Recommended minimum number of sessions: Two. Do the second session sometime within the following six days. On the days you don't do this meditation, use #1, #5, or #7 as the basis for your daily meditation while utilizing everything you've learned so far.

> Total duration so far, assuming you meditate *every* day:
> **Fifteen weeks**

Check off each box or write the dates of your sessions inside to help you track your progress.

15. When longing and feeling stuck

Recommended minimum number of sessions: Two. Do the second session sometime within the following six days. On the days you don't do this meditation, use #1, #5, or #7 as the basis for your daily meditation while utilizing everything you've learned so far.

> Total duration so far, assuming you meditate *every* day:
> **Sixteen weeks**

Check off each box or write the dates of your sessions inside to help you track your progress.

16. Emotions in the body (lying down)

Recommended minimum number of sessions: Seven.

Total duration so far, assuming you meditate *every* day:
Seventeen weeks

Check off each box or write the dates of your sessions inside to help you track your progress.

17. Positive person who has passed away

Recommended minimum number of sessions: Two. Do the second session sometime within the following six days. On the days you don't do this meditation, use #1, #5, #7, or #16 as the basis for your daily meditation while utilizing everything you've learned so far.

Total duration so far, assuming you meditate *every* day:
Eighteen weeks

Check off each box or write the dates of your sessions inside to help you track your progress.

The Heart Series

18. Facing a negative person from one's past

Recommended minimum number of sessions: One. For the six days following, use #1, #5, #7, or #16 as the basis for your daily meditation while utilizing everything you've learned so far.

Total duration so far, assuming you meditate *every* day:
Nineteen weeks

Check off each box or write the dates of your sessions inside to help you track your progress.

19. Apologizing to people from one's past

Recommended minimum number of sessions: One. For the six days following, use #1, #5, #7, or #16 as the basis for your daily meditation while utilizing everything you've learned so far.

Total duration so far, assuming you meditate *every* day:
Twenty weeks

Check off each box or write the dates of your sessions inside to help you track your progress.

20. Life celebration

Recommended minimum number of sessions: One. For the six days following, use #1, #5, #7, or #16 as the basis for your daily meditation while utilizing everything you've learned so far.

Total duration so far, assuming you meditate *every* day:
Twenty-one weeks

Check off each box or write the dates of your sessions inside to help you track your progress.

21. Body networks

Recommended minimum number of sessions: Two. For the five days following, use #1, #5, #7, or #16 as the basis for your daily meditation while utilizing everything you've learned so far.

Total duration so far, assuming you meditate *every* day:
Twenty-two weeks

Check off each box or write the dates of your sessions inside to help you track your progress.

The Heart Series

22. Sending love to all parts of one's body

Recommended minimum number of sessions: Three, spread throughout the week. On the in-between days, use #1, #5, #7, or #16 as the basis for your daily meditation while utilizing everything you've learned so far.

Total duration so far, assuming you meditate *every* day:
Twenty-three weeks

Check off each box or write the dates of your sessions inside to help you track your progress.

23. Loving-kindness

Recommended minimum number of sessions: Three, spread throughout the week. On the in-between days, use #1, #5, #7, or #16 as the basis for your daily meditation while utilizing everything you've learned so far.

Total duration so far, assuming you meditate *every* day:
Twenty-four weeks

Check off each box or write the dates of your sessions inside to help you track your progress.

THE TRANSPERSONAL SERIES

24. Sending love to the Earth and stars

Recommended minimum number of sessions: One. For the six days following, use #1, #5, #7, or #16 as the basis for your daily meditation while utilizing everything you've learned so far.

Total duration so far, assuming you meditate *every* day:
Twenty-five weeks

Check off each box or write the dates of your sessions inside to help you track your progress.

25. Communicating with the other side

Recommended minimum number of sessions: Two. For the five days following, use #1, #5, #7, or #16 as the basis for your daily meditation while utilizing everything you've learned so far.

Total duration so far, assuming you meditate *every* day:
Twenty-six weeks

Check off each box or write the dates of your sessions inside to help you track your progress.

The Transpersonal Series

26. Cosmic Flow

Recommended minimum number of sessions: Two, spread apart in the next week. For the other five days, use #1, #5, #7, or #16 as the basis for your daily meditation while utilizing everything you've learned so far.

Total duration so far, assuming you meditate *every* day:
Twenty-seven weeks

Check off each box or write the dates of your sessions inside to help you track your progress.

THE SPACE AND ENERGY SERIES

27. Sinking into the space of the Earth

Recommended minimum number of sessions: Seven.

> Total duration so far, assuming you meditate *every* day:
> **Twenty-eight weeks**

Check off each box or write the dates of your sessions inside to help you track your progress.

28. Absorbing energy from the Earth (lying down)

Recommended minimum number of sessions: Seven.

> Total duration so far, assuming you meditate *every* day:
> **Twenty-nine weeks**

Check off each box or write the dates of your sessions inside to help you track your progress.

The Space and Energy Series

29. Mindfulness of space in the body

Recommended minimum number of sessions: Fourteen.

Total duration so far, assuming you meditate *every* day:
Thirty-one weeks

Check off each box or write the dates of your sessions inside to help you track your progress.

30. Space and energy

Recommended minimum number of sessions: Fourteen.

Total duration so far, assuming you meditate *every* day:
Thirty-three weeks

Check off each box or write the dates of your sessions inside to help you track your progress.

31. Absorbing Earth energy (lying down then sitting up)

Recommended minimum number of sessions: Fourteen.

Total duration so far, assuming you meditate *every* day:
Thirty-five weeks

Check off each box or write the dates of your sessions inside to help you track your progress.

32. Space beyond the body

Recommended minimum number of sessions: Seven, **alternating** with #1 <u>over the next two weeks</u>.

Total duration so far, assuming you meditate *every* day:
Thirty-seven weeks

Check off each box or write the dates of your sessions inside to help you track your progress.

THE DEEP PEACE SERIES

33. Clarifying awareness

Recommended minimum number of sessions: Fourteen.

By the eighth session of this technique, you should be able to do this meditation without Sean's guidance, utilizing all applicable concepts learned in earlier meditations for dealing with tension and distraction.

Total duration so far, assuming you meditate *every* day:
Thirty-nine weeks

Check off each box or write the dates of your sessions inside to help you track your progress.

34. Precise focus

Recommended minimum number of sessions: Twenty-one.

By the eighth session of this technique, you should be able to do this meditation without Sean's guidance, utilizing all applicable concepts learned in earlier meditations for dealing with tension and distraction.

Total duration so far, assuming you meditate *every* day:
Forty-two weeks

Check off each box or write the dates of your sessions inside to help you track your progress.

The Deep Peace Series

35. Three parts of the breath

Recommended minimum number of sessions: Twenty-one.

By the eighth session of this technique, you should be able to do this meditation without Sean's guidance, utilizing all applicable concepts learned in earlier meditations for dealing with tension and distraction.

Total duration so far, assuming you meditate *every* day:
Forty-five weeks

Check off each box or write the dates of your sessions inside to help you track your progress.

36. Moving from the breath to pleasant sensations

Recommended minimum number of sessions: Twenty-one.

By the eighth session of this technique, you should be able to do this meditation without Sean's guidance, utilizing all applicable concepts learned in earlier meditations for dealing with tension and distraction.

Total duration so far, assuming you meditate *every* day:
Forty-eight weeks

Check off each box or write the dates of your sessions inside to help you track your progress.

The Deep Peace Series

37. Moving from pleasant sensations to contentment

Recommended minimum number of sessions: Twenty-eight (one month).

By the eighth session of this technique, you should be able to do this meditation without Sean's guidance, utilizing all applicable concepts learned in earlier meditations for dealing with tension, distraction, and letting go into stillness.

Total duration so far, assuming you meditate *every* day:
Fifty-two weeks

Check off each box or write the dates of your sessions inside to help you track your progress.

38. Deep peace

Recommended minimum number of sessions: Twenty-eight (one month). These sessions are much longer than usual, and you should make every effort to complete the whole session during this period. Of course, if you can't, then shorten it as needed. **Meditating for a shorter period is better than not meditating at all.**

By the eighth session of this technique, you should be able to do this meditation without Sean's guidance, utilizing all applicable concepts learned in earlier meditations for dealing with tension and distraction, and letting go into peace.

Total duration so far, assuming you meditate *every* day:
Fifty-six weeks

Check off each box or write the dates of your sessions inside to help you track your progress.

THE NATURE OF MIND SERIES

39. Nature of thoughts Part 1

Recommended minimum number of sessions: Three, alternating with #1 or any other techniques you'd like to do over the following week.

Total duration so far, assuming you meditate *every* day:
Fifty-seven weeks

Check off each box or write the dates of your sessions inside to help you track your progress.

40. Nature of thoughts Part 2

Recommended minimum number of sessions: Fourteen. After the third or fourth session, you should be able to guide your own sessions for this period without Sean's video.

Total duration so far, assuming you meditate *every* day:
Fifty-nine weeks

Check off each box or write the dates of your sessions inside to help you track your progress.

41. Nature of the body as the five elements

Recommended minimum number of sessions: Fourteen. After the third or fourth session, you should be able to guide your own sessions for this period without Sean's video.

Total duration so far, assuming you meditate *every* day:
Sixty-one weeks

Check off each box or write the dates of your sessions inside to help you track your progress.

42. Nature of feeling-response

Recommended minimum number of sessions: Fourteen. After the third or fourth session, you should be able to guide your own sessions for this period without Sean's video.

Total duration so far, assuming you meditate *every* day:
Sixty-three weeks

Check off each box or write the dates of your sessions inside to help you track your progress.

The Nature of Mind Series

43. Nature of emotions

Recommended minimum number of sessions: Fourteen. After the third or fourth session, you should be able to guide your own sessions for this period without Sean's video.

If you're interested in eventually practicing the meditations from the final series, Union Practice/Sexual Yoga, it is crucial for you to become proficient at this practice. On days when you experience strong emotions, positive or negative, take advantage of them as opportunities to train using this method.

Manufacturing emotions (as is done in the online video) is for teaching the method. After learning it, you must apply it when true and powerful emotions arise.

Total duration so far, assuming you meditate *every* day:
Sixty-five weeks

Check off each box or write the dates of your sessions inside to help you track your progress.

44. Nature of sense perceptions

Recommended minimum number of sessions: Three, alternating with #1 or any other techniques you'd like to do over the following week.

Total duration so far, assuming you meditate *every* day:
Sixty-six weeks

Check off each box or write the dates of your sessions inside to help you track your progress.

The Nature of Mind Series

45. Looking at the looker

Recommended minimum number of sessions: Fourteen, alternating with #1 or any other techniques you'd like to do over the following four weeks. Most of these sessions should be self-guided based on everything you've learned so far.

Like the note for #43, if you're interested in eventually training in Union Practice/Sexual Yoga, becoming proficient at this meditation is essential. It is unlikely that the minimum recommended sessions will be enough to prepare you for those practices, so be prepared to continue developing yourself more before delving into Sexual Yoga.

Total duration so far, assuming you meditate *every* day:
Sixty-eight weeks

Check off each box or write the dates of your sessions inside to help you track your progress.

46. Blending awareness and space

Recommended minimum number of sessions: Fourteen.

Total duration so far, assuming you meditate *every* day:
Seventy weeks

Check off each box or write the dates of your sessions inside to help you track your progress.

47. Resting in the nature of awareness

The recommended minimum number of sessions of meditation #47 before moving on to the Visionary series or the Union/Sexual Yoga series: Twenty-eight.

After the third or fourth session, you should be able to do them without Sean's guidance or by referring to them only once in a while.

Total duration so far, assuming you meditate *every* day:
Seventy-four weeks

Check off each box or write the dates of your sessions inside to help you track your progress.

The Nature of Mind Series

At this point, #47 could become your main, ongoing practice, as could the meditations from the Deep Peace series. Or you could decide which of the forty-seven meditations to do on any given day according to your inspiration, curiosity, and needs.

Therefore, there are *no more little boxes* for you to mark your progress at this point. There is no finish line, and no goal to reach. The recommended schedule was merely guidance to help you prepare for this point.

From now on, your meditation practice will serve to maintain and deepen your connection with your deeper awareness and the world around you.

However, there are still several meditations left to learn if you are so inclined. These are in the Visionary series, the Sleep and Dream series, Meditation on the External Elements, and Union Practice/Sexual Yoga, listed in the following pages.

Please respect the importance of having done at least twenty-eight sessions of #47, and at least seventy-four weeks of total training (assuming you meditate every day) *before* attempting the following practices.

As for the rest, without having strongly established oneself in discerning the nature of mind, and without developing stillness and clarity, these practices will only cause you to get lost in distracting thoughts, fantasies, and excess or misplaced pride.

Without sufficient preparation, it may be difficult, if not impossible, to properly relate to the very subtle visions perceived during the candle gazing and sun gazing practices. It will also be extremely challenging to engage in the sexual yoga practices properly.

The risk of doing them too soon is that you'll experience these meditations in the wrong way, from the wrong state of consciousness. Then, when you attempt to practice them at their appropriate time (after at least seventy-four weeks of training), you'll refer to your memory of your first time looking at them which can block or blur the intended, authentic experience, at least for a while.

THE VISIONARY SERIES

48. Sky gazing
49. Candle gazing
50. Sun gazing

THE SLEEP AND DREAM SERIES

51. Awareness of dreams in meditation
52. Awareness of awareness itself while sleeping

Note: The sleep and dream practices in the *Path of the Golden Teacher* online program differ from commonly known lucid dreaming and dream yoga techniques.

If you are interested in learning how to lucid dream, you can find step-by-step instructions in the following books:

- the second edition of my memoir *Renegade Mystic*

- *Renegade Mystic's Concise Instructions for Lucid Dreaming and the Out of Body Experience: A Companion to the First Edition of Renegade Mystic.*

The Final Series

I also offer an online video course on lucid dreaming and out-of-body experiences at www.MindPossible.com.

MEDITATION ON THE EXTERNAL ELEMENTS

53. Wind
54. Fire
55. Water
56. Earth

UNION PRACTICE/SEXUAL YOGA

57. Union practice/sexual yoga

In case it's helpful for you to decide whether to do the *Path of the Golden Teacher* online guided meditation program, reviews from the first meditators who used it are in Part Five. Also, several of the videos in the online program are available to watch as a free preview. This is to give you a sense of how the sessions are guided.

PART TWO

THE PSYCHEDELIC JOURNEY

INTRODUCTION TO THE PSYCHEDELIC JOURNEY

    With or without having trained in meditation, the psychedelic journey can be one of the most transformative and fulfilling experiences of one's life. As you have probably already heard, journeying has profound spiritual and psychological effects.

    Spiritually, it can provide insights and understandings at an experiential level. For those whose understanding has been limited to what is written in ancient texts or parroted during religious services, this is their opportunity to see things with their own eyes. It grants them the power and conviction to either confirm what they've been told to believe or question it without apology.

    Psychologically, journeying has been described as achieving in several hours what would take months or years to accomplish in therapy. A single dose of psilocybin can greatly reduce treatment-resistant depression for months, eliminating the need for daily pharmaceutical use.

    Psychedelics have also been effective in mitigating various types of addiction, healing trauma, reducing anxiety, and boosting creativity. Artists and engineers alike have developed new concepts and products thanks to their use of psychedelics.

But psychedelics come with risks, and everyone should be aware of those risks before taking a journey. To help you understand those risks, I've written the chapters *Contraindications for Psychedelics* and *Cautionary Tales*.

Many first-time journeyers are only aware of options like paying a therapist to sit for them, paying to be guided by a shaman, or paying to journey with a room full of strangers. They might not even consider the possibility of journeying alone or with a trusted friend and the benefits of doing so. Therefore, to help you empower yourself to journey alone, I've written the chapter *How to Journey Alone and Why*.

Some readers might prefer to have someone watching over them just to be safe and comfortable. The final chapter of this section, *How to Journey with a Sitter* offers guidance on how to sit for someone. You can share this chapter with a friend who is willing to sit for you to help them feel confident in assisting you. You don't need to pay a professional to have a good experience.

After reading the list of contraindications, you may decide you are an appropriate candidate for using a psychedelic. You should know there is still the risk of having a challenging experience, otherwise known as a bad trip. According to some studies, that risk can be as high as ten percent. Education and forewarning can be effective in reducing that risk. The chapter *Preparation* is self-explanatory. After that, *Your Journey* gives a general description of what you can expect from the moment you consume your dose to feeling back to normal several hours later.

In a sense, the journey is only the first part of healing. The days, months, and years afterward are when much of the important work happens. This is called *integration*, and the chapter by the same name will offer guidance on how to do that.

Introduction to the Psychedelic Journey

As you can tell, taking a psychedelic is much more than just taking a substance and tripping out. It's a significant event in one's life. Some would regard it as a sacred initiation. Others would call it a life-saving measure.

No matter what, it should be treated with respect. I hope the following chapters gives you the knowledge, confidence, and encouragement to transform your life this way.

CONTRAINDICATIONS FOR PSYCHEDELICS

The following are reasons *not* to use psilocybin or other psychedelics. You will remember that some of these are included in Part One's *Contraindications for Meditation*.

High blood pressure or other cardiovascular issues

Psilocybin can increase your blood pressure and heart rate. For those with pre-existing conditions, this can be problematic or worse. You should consult with your physician before deciding to use the psychedelic.

Contraindications for Psychedelics

Mushroom allergy

If you are allergic to mushrooms in general, you will experience the same immune response to psilocybin. This can range from mild or moderate symptoms like rash or upset stomach to severe symptoms like anaphylaxis, which can be lethal.

Even if you do not have a mushroom allergy, it can be prudent to try a microdosing regimen before taking a journey dose. If a microdose causes symptoms like severe headache or gastrointestinal discomfort, it may be best to avoid psilocybin in larger quantities.

Remember that a journey will last several hours, and that's a very long time to feel ill. This could lead to a terrible overall experience.

Strong fear about taking psilocybin, difficulty letting go, or potential to react violently while under stress

If you feel significant fear or anxiety about consuming psilocybin or other psychedelics, you should not do so. Those emotions will only become more pronounced during the journey leading to a potentially terrifying experience. Also, difficulty letting go can block the experience or at least prevent it from unfolding naturally, which can be stressful and confusing.

If you have been known to react to stress or anger through physical acts like throwing or scattering household objects, breaking things, or pushing, shoving, or yelling at other people, you should not take the psychedelic.

Being under the age of 25

The brain is still under significant development until around the age of 25. It's best to abstain from psychedelics in early adulthood to ensure good brain health and personality development.

Also, people are particularly at risk of developing psychosis or other mental health conditions between the ages of 18 and 25. Taking a psychedelic at that age increases that risk. But, keep in mind mental disorders can occur at any age.

Pregnancy or breastfeeding

Studies have *not* been done to determine if taking psilocybin poses a risk during pregnancy or breastfeeding.[20] However, it is prudent to be as safe as possible and abstain from taking psychedelics while pregnant or breastfeeding.

Due to compromised balance, mobility, and altered perceptions while under the influence, the mother is at risk of falling or other kinds of accidents while journeying.

Suicidal ideation or previous suicide attempts

Psychedelics amplify emotions and thought patterns. Therefore, if you are prone to the following then it's likely those or other suicide-related thoughts and emotions will arise during the journey, and with significant intensity:

- rumination
- existential crisis
- loss of meaning

---

[20] National Library of Medicine. (May 2023) Mother to Baby Fact Sheets. Psilocybin Mushrooms ("Magic Mushrooms"). https://www.ncbi.nlm.nih.gov/books/NBK582810/

Contraindications for Psychedelics

- feeling directionless
- loneliness
- depression
- helplessness
- profound and unacknowledged anger about harm or injustice that has been inflicted on you.
- persistent desire to punish someone or make them acknowledge how they harmed you - but are powerless to do so

SUICIDE HOTLINE

If you're in the United States and are having thoughts of suicide, please **call or text 988** for help or visit **https://988lifeline.org**.

If you're outside the U.S., please look up your local suicide prevention services and make sure you know how to reach them should you disregard the contraindication and use a psychedelic.

Bipolar disorder, schizophrenia, dissociative conditions, or a history of experiencing psychotic breaks

Psychedelics increase the risk of triggering or activating any of these in someone with a pre-existing condition. Remember that in a sense, the psychedelic journey is a planned and temporary departure from the normal state of mind and from ordinary reality which **can** be safe for those **without** mental health risks, symptoms, or conditions.

Taking the following medications:

- SSRIs such as: fluoxetine (Prozac), paroxetine (Paxil), sertraline (Zoloft)
- trazodone (Desyrel)
- Lithium
- tricyclic antidepressants such as amitriptyline (Elavil)
- Haloperidol
- MAOIs such as linezolid (Zyvox), rasagiline (Azilect), or St. John's Wort

Psilocybin and other psychedelics interact with neurotransmitter receptors in the brain and elsewhere, particularly related to serotonin. Various pharmaceuticals interact with those same receptors. Therefore, by using a psychedelic at the same time one is using a pharmaceutical, it's possible to:

- Block the medication or decrease its effectiveness.

- Block the psychedelic (this is most noticeable when nothing or very little occurs after consuming a journey dose).

- Overwhelm the nervous system with serotonin, causing serotonin toxicity, also known as *serotonin syndrome,* which can have severe consequences including death.

Many recent online articles and interviews report the risk of serotonin syndrome to be very low for psilocybin. But for those who use an MAOI, the risk is significant with DMT. Regardless, anyone taking these medications should consult with their doctor before using any psychedelics.

Contraindications for Psychedelics

Some people look to microdosing as a substitute for pharmaceuticals, especially if they are only using a low dose for issues like sleep disturbance. It may be prudent to taper off the medication before starting a microdosing regimen. However, some people report positive outcomes while microdosing simultaneously with low doses of a pharmaceutical.[21]

Tapering or quitting a pharmaceutical medication cold turkey can be extremely difficult and have negative repercussions. Therefore, some people opt to use both simultaneously first, and then taper off their medication after microdosing for several months.

You should consult with your doctor about the best way for you to proceed.

The following website also has information about tapering: www.SurvivingAntidepressants.org.

Legal restrictions in your area

You should become aware of the regional (state) and national laws regarding growing, extracting, possessing, sharing, selling, and using psychedelics.

Not all psychedelics are regarded equally in the eyes of the law, so you should be specific when researching the one you plan to use. Consequences of breaking the law may include monetary fines, imprisonment, and loss of professional licensure.

---

[21] Hasty, Marie. "Psilocybin and Ssris: A Talk with Dr. Erica Zelfand, Nd Psychedelic Support." *Psychedelic Support · Psychedelic Support*, 28 Mar. 2024, https://www.psychedelic.support/resources/psilocybin-and-ssris/. (See Case Study #4)

SUPPORT FOR CHALLENGING PSYCHEDELIC EXPERIENCES

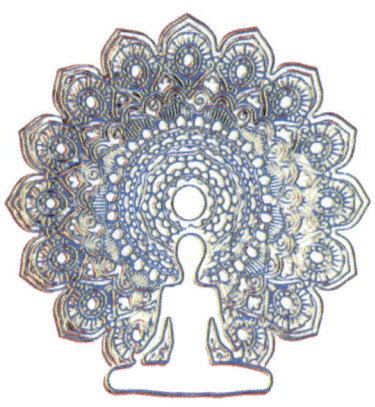

The following websites offer support, guidance, and information about dealing with psychological and emotional difficulties during and after a challenging psychedelic journey:

- www.FiresideProject.org

- www.ZendoProject.org/resources/

CAUTIONARY TALES

The cautionary tales below are included because they can prepare you in ways a list of contraindications or suggestions for safe use can't.

Sam

Sam flew across the country to experience a psychedelic journey in Colorado. He invested the time, money, and energy to do so because he was at a crossroads in his life. He sought insights and inspiration for deciding what to do next.

He let his sitter know he didn't have any of the listed contraindications and he felt confident about taking a normal dose.

One hour after drinking his psilocybin, he didn't feel any effects other than periodic yawning. Sam chose to take a booster dose at that point. But there were no additional effects from the psilocybin save for the appearance of tears. It was only by chance that Sam's sitter noticed his tears because Sam wasn't crying or giving other indicators of sadness.

During what would've normally been the post-journey integration session, Sam and his sitter discussed possible explanations for the disappointing experience.

It turned out that Sam had experienced nearly a decade of extreme psychological stress. Obtaining an advanced degree, working in a high-intensity environment, experiencing vicarious trauma daily at work, and grieving the deaths of several friends had left Sam utterly burned out.

The sitter's first theory is that Sam's neuroreceptors are, like Sam, burned out due to extreme levels of daily stress, rendering them incapable of interacting with the psychedelic in the usual way.

This theory isn't scientific but sounds plausible.

The sitter also has a second theory. It's possible that although Sam made the outward effort to experience a journey, deep inside he was unable to open to the experience. His subconscious need for control and predictability may have been so strong that his mind prevented the psychedelic's effects.

A third and most likely theory is that Sam lied about not taking SSRIs, and they had blocked the psilocybin's effect.

Before saying goodbye, the sitter recommended that Sam seek professional therapy, take measures to reduce his stress and adopt a daily self-care regimen. It will probably take Sam several years to recover from everything he's been through.

Christina

Christina grew up in a cult that her parents had joined before her birth. Their beliefs greatly differed from those of mainstream religions. Because Christina took a job after leaving home that exposed her to television, the internet, and conversations with outsiders, she was exposed to other perspectives.

At first, this felt liberating. Though she was of adult age, she was still at the young stage of developing her personality and differentiating from her parents.

Her curiosity and openness to new ideas were also a cause for stress. She discovered there are many choices of what to believe ranging from well-established religions to spiritual-but-not-religious teachings to extreme, fear-based conspiracies.

Just when she thought she finally found something new to believe in, she'd hear somebody else's ideas on social media and submerge herself in them until something more intriguing came along.

Christina didn't realize how vulnerable she was. After being told exactly what to believe most of her life, she intentionally discarded those ideas and sought a suitable replacement. Therefore, she was a blank slate.

She didn't understand how exposed she was by watching YouTube videos and listening to various podcasts for several hours each day.

She felt confused, distraught, and desperate to find a belief system she could adopt for the rest of her life.

There was another challenge for Christina, though. She had also discovered psychedelics. But as provocative and empowering as they seemed, her journeys didn't help.

Half the time, they wiped out whatever sense of self she'd developed since leaving her family. This forced her to start over the only way she knew how, by listening to more online influencers and adopting their points of view without using her discernment. She had never been taught how to use discernment, let alone common sense.

The other times she journeyed, she experienced visions of suffering in a hell-like environment. These were terrifying and extremely stressful. She wondered if they foretold the retribution awaiting her for contradicting her family's beliefs.

This left her torn, unsure of what to believe, vulnerable, and with an incomplete sense of self.

Christina should abstain from psychedelics until she matures and develops a stable identity for herself. This process can take many years and can't be rushed.

She should also reduce her social media consumption and seek guidance for developing discernment, perhaps with the help of a counselor.

Joy, Anna, and Michelle

Joy and Anna worked together and had become close friends over the last few years. A couple of months ago, they met Michelle, whom they had lunch with several times. She seemed like a nice enough person, but their conversations were never very personal.

One day, Joy and Anna told Michelle they planned to rent a house in the mountains and take turns sitting for each other so they could journey with psilocybin. Michelle eagerly responded, "I'd love to do that! Can I come?" Not wanting to reject their new friend, Joy and Anna agreed to let her accompany them for the weekend.

Joy and Anna had arranged to meet with an experienced friend to explain how they could support each other without hiring a professional sitter. Michelle was invited to the meeting but let them know she couldn't make it.

Everything seemed fine until they drove to the house that weekend. In the car, Michelle was unusually withdrawn. Then, she began making random remarks about how they could die that weekend.

Joy and Anna did their best to laugh away her strange comments. But after unpacking and settling in, Michelle's behavior worsened. She ushered them into the living room for an "important meeting" to discuss what she'd intuited in the car, that they would either die that weekend or on the car ride home.

Cautionary Tales

Still, Joy and Anna were gracious and acted as sitters that day while Michelle journeyed in her room. When Joy checked in on her, Michelle verbally lashed out at her, screaming for her to get out. Later, Anna checked on her and noticed her clothes and belongings strewn about the room. Michelle mumbled a bit, but Anna couldn't understand what she said. Michelle didn't sound like herself.

When Michelle's journey was finished, she seemed introspective and calm. But as Joy drank her psilocybin (it was her turn), Michelle repeated her fearful comments about everyone dying.

Joy was already on edge about Michelle's behavior and felt more aggravated because she knew Michelle's words could affect her journey. Fortunately, she didn't experience a bad trip because of it. Instead, she was wound up so tight it reduced the psilocybin's effectiveness. Simply put, her journey was disappointing.

Anna was already too nervous to take her dose. She chose not to, and when Joy was ready, she drove the three of them home.

Later Joy and Anna reported this to their other friend, wondering what went wrong. After reviewing the events, several things were made clear:

- It was risky to invite someone they barely knew to journey with them.

- Michelle's unwillingness to receive guidance and preparation with Anna and Joy was a red flag.

- Michelle's strange behavior in the car and upon arriving at the house were warning signs that she was mentally unstable. This was sufficient justification to cancel the whole event.

- Joy's inability to fully let go into her journey was understandable. How could she have possibly felt safe and comfortable in that environment knowing how Michelle was behaving?

- Anna's instinct to cancel her journey was correct. If she had pushed on, she might have had a similar experience to Joy's, or worse, an overwhelming and frightful journey.

Gabriel

Gabriel hired the services of a professional sitter. The arrangement was for Gabriel to stay in a guest room at the sitter's home.

As Gabriel unpacked and settled into his room, he noticed something felt familiar, but he couldn't pin it down.

It wasn't until after his psychedelic journey began that he realized what it was. Instead of lying down with a blindfold over his eyes, he opted to sit up in bed and look out at the room.

Staring at the worn wooden dresser near the foot of the bed, he realized it was the same model that had been in his bedroom when he was in foster care many years ago. It was during that time of his life, as a boy, when an older foster sibling repeatedly assaulted him in his room.

Triggered by seeing the dresser, Gabriel was forced to endure recurring memories from that time of his life for much of his journey.

There's no way that Gabriel could have predicted this would happen. Even if he had visited the room beforehand, the dresser might not have triggered the memory then.

This account is shared as a reminder of how beneficial it can be to journey in a familiar and comfortable environment like one's home. It reduces unpredictable risks.

Cautionary Tales

Frank and Josie

Frank and Josie are a retired couple who've always been curious about trying psychedelics. They decided to rent a condo in a touristy mountain town to make it an extra special event.

The condo was perfect, with a nice kitchen and a private yard. It was also situated near a paved walkway that followed a creek past other condos, restaurants, and shops.

They drank their psilocybin an hour after having a light lunch and enjoyed their trips in separate bedrooms.

They seemed to finish their journeys around the same time several hours later. The sun was beginning to set but it was still warm outside, so they decided to take a stroll along the creek-side path into town. They were in a wonderful mood, and both commented on how the crystalline water, golden aspen leaves, and cobalt sky above looked more beautiful than ever.

Along the way, Frank spotted a public restroom and since nature was calling, he let Josie know he needed a couple of minutes. Josie was happy to wander around nearby.

While Frank was in the bathroom, he heard angry yelling outside. It was Josie! "Who is she screaming at?" he wondered. By the time he finished up and stepped outside, the yelling had stopped.

He found Josie twenty yards down the path. She was observing a nearby herd of elk grazing by the creek.

Frank asked, "What happened? Who were you screaming at?" Josie seemed tense but relatively calm.

"Some jackass was standing way too close to the herd and upsetting them. I think he was drunk; he had a beer in his hand."

"Okay, but why did you scream at him? You're lucky he didn't come at you!" Frank noticed the man off in the distance, walking away.

"You know how much I love nature. That guy was totally disrespectful to these poor animals, and I can't stand it when people do that. Not on my watch, mister! No way!"

Frank and Josie decided to turn around and head back to the condo. After a couple of minutes, Frank asked, "Do you think you might still be tripping?"

"I guess I'm still feeling it a little bit," she replied. "I don't think I would've yelled at a stranger like that, let alone a drunk man, if I were completely sober. I just felt super protective of the herd."

In this case, Frank and Josie took a risk by going out in public at an unknown locale after their journey. It's common to feel extra sensitive after the obvious effects have worn off.

They would've done better by playing it safe and hanging out in their private backyard instead of walking into town.

Ben and friends

Ben and four friends had rented a mountain home through one of those shared-economy websites. They planned to stay there for two nights.

Ben had just come to be with his friends, but not to journey with them. Two planned to journey on the evening of their arrival. The other two would journey the next day. They'd all leave together on the morning of the third day.

By the looks of the parking lot, Ben guessed his four friends had already arrived and were inside. But as he pulled into the driveway, he noticed a stranger entering the front door. From Ben's viewpoint, it looked like a two-story home.

When Ben entered, he found his four friends quietly sitting on a couple of couches. They looked nervous. But the stranger was nowhere to be seen.

"Hi everyone! I just saw a guy walk in here. Who was that? Where did he go?" Ben asked.

One of his friends replied, "We have no idea who he is. He just walked in here, said 'hi' and that he was a neighbor. He came to access the owners' wi-fi and then went up those stairs to talk to them." She pointed to a recessed staircase leading to the upper level.

This was strange. The property listing said they'd have the whole place to themselves. This was important to them because they knew they needed privacy to feel safe while journeying, even if a friend was there to protect them.

But it turned out the upper floor was occupied by the owners, and apparently, the neighbor was accustomed to entering the lower floor without warning to visit them.

One of the friends called the owners and asked to discuss what just happened. The husband came down, oblivious to why his renters needed his attention.

Ben described the situation. The owner apologized profusely and offered them a discount for their trouble. He also offered to change the electronic door code so nobody else could enter the property. Then he returned upstairs so the friends could think about their next move.

They already felt a breach of trust because the owner misled them with the online listing. They did not, in fact, have the property all to themselves. Their privacy had been violated.

What if other neighbors were also accustomed to entering the home without notice? Even if the owner changed the door code, people might still come knocking or peering through the windows.

Fortunately, the first two friends hadn't yet consumed their psilocybin when the stranger walked in. That could've initiated a horrible trip.

The group decided the location wasn't appropriate for journeying They notified the owner of their cancellation and left. They notified the website which hosted the listing about the discrepancy and got a full refund.

Leaving was the right decision. It was a difficult choice because they'd dedicated a whole weekend to this event, and everyone looked forward to a fruitful journey. But they knew it wasn't worth the risk and postponed instead.

Don't surrender your autonomy to a chemical effect.

This isn't an anecdote, but it's important to consider. Some people, either on their own or because they belong to a tradition that teaches them this, attach selfhood to a substance. For example, ayahuasca is often referred to as Mama Ayahuasca and some people feel like "she" offers them advice and direction during a journey. This is appropriate for those who belong to the cultural group that traditionally holds this view.

But what about you? Were you born into this type of culture? Or is it a choice you're making?

Whether using ayahuasca, psilocybin, or anything else, be careful not to regard psychedelically-originated messages or symbolism as unquestionable or inviolable. The ideas that come during a journey could be just plain wrong, and mere byproducts of your inherent creativity.

It's alright to question the feelings and ideas that arise during a journey, and to wait weeks, months, or longer before acting on them. Acting hastily can have disastrous effects.

Please remember you don't have to surrender your power to an anthropomorphized substance, a person, or to a set of spiritual beliefs that you haven't consciously adopted.

HOW TO JOURNEY ALONE AND WHY

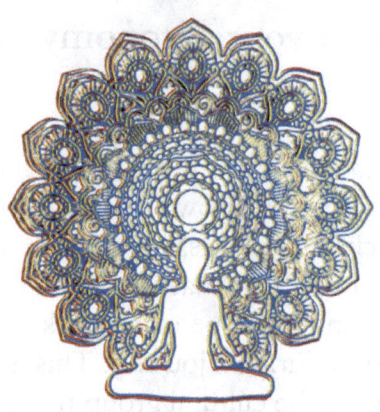

Sitters, therapists, and shamans are increasingly advertising their services of watching over you while you journey for psychological and spiritual support.

Regulatory agencies, schools, mental health professionals, and plant-medicine-based churches are cashing in on what is quickly becoming an extremely lucrative service industry.

The concept of journeying alone is relatively unheard of online and may seem frightening or dangerous to some. Commercial interests would naturally prefer public perception to remain that way.

Let's empower ourselves by considering how advertising works in the supermarket. Looking at the produce section filled with nutritious fruits and vegetables, we notice they don't come with fancy labels or flashy advertising. They also cost far less than processed food stuffed into plastic bags and cardboard boxes.

Path of the Golden Teacher

We don't see ads on social media for apples, sweet potatoes, and broccoli, do we?

Journeying alone is like buying produce while paying for someone to watch over you is like purchasing processed food.

Like processed food, the service is expensive because the seller must spend money on advertising to convince you theirs is the best way to go. And in some cases, it is.

Many people will prefer to have someone with them especially if it's their first time or if they are particularly vulnerable for some reason. For some people, journeying alone does present a considerable risk.

And for those with disposable income, affordability is not an obstacle. If they strongly prefer to have someone else in the room with them, why shouldn't they hire a professional sitter?

But the psychedelic underground is and has always been comprised of self-trained psychonauts who, out of financial reasons, personal preference, or because they inherited the necessary folk wisdom, have always journeyed alone.

And since journeying alone isn't a sellable service, you'll never see an ad for it online or on TV.

Learning to journey alone can be just as fruitful and, in some ways, safer than paying a professional to sit with you.

By growing your own psilocybin (see Part Three to learn how), you'll be able to decide for yourself how much or how little to take, and how often. As you'll read later, my recommendation is to start with a smaller dose and carefully work your way up in future journeys based on your experience.

If you were to pay a service provider, they would determine the dose for you, hopefully with your input. And since you paid so much money for it, both they and you would want to ensure you had a significant experience. The risk is it could be a larger dose than necessary which could lead to an uncomfortable or even harmful experience.

When you have your own supply of psilocybin, there's no rush and no pressure to gamble on dosage. You don't have to treat it like a once-in-a-lifetime opportunity. Instead, it can be a lifelong relationship based on careful experimentation.

In terms of safety, the best place to journey is at home. There, you are fully in control of your environment. You have the choice of journeying in bed, on the couch, in your meditation space, or your backyard (assuming guaranteed privacy).

And naturally, all these spaces will feel cozy, familiar, and safe. You don't even have to commit to only one of those choices. Your ability to move from one room to another during your journey is a bonus.

You also know where the bathroom is and have it all to yourself. You'll have easy access to your preferred foods since your kitchen is nearby. If you call a friend for help or simply for companionship, they already know where you live so reaching you will be easy for them.

If you live with someone else, knowing they're in another room and can call out to them if you need immediate assistance can also be supportive.

Journeying by yourself removes the risk of a negative or even harmful interaction with a stranger. In the first couple of years of psilocybin's decriminalization in certain cities and states, there have already been reports of sitters, therapists, and shamans behaving improperly toward their clients while they were vulnerable (journeying), including acts of sexual assault.

Even minor conditions can hurt your experience. For example, your sitter being in a foul mood on the day of your journey, a stranger substituting for your sitter because they called in sick that day, the sitter coloring your experience with their belief system instead of yours or being forced to listen to a musical playlist or ritual songs that don't suit you.

Another option is to journey with a group of strangers. Remember that with psilocybin, everything is amplified, including emotional responses. For me, crying is a highly personal and delicate event. I don't like the idea of automatically permitting a room full of strangers to witness me in such a vulnerable state, especially if they're also under the influence.

And what if I'm crying, but the person next to me is having a five-minute-long laughter fit? And what if someone else starts screaming in anger because their journey revived the memory of a childhood trauma?

I understand that one benefit of journeying in a group is the opportunity to have an integration session together afterward. After being so vulnerable and witnessing each other during the journey it's natural to want to share insights and gratitude afterward.

But is it healthy in all cases? There's therapeutic processing and then there's people with permeable boundaries bonding over the emotional hook of experiencing extreme states together.

A healthy community can be healing. An unhealthy community is harmful. When a person signs up to experience a journey with a room full of strangers and integrate with them afterward, they're taking a chance on the character of the other participants and the leader.

It can seem enticing to join a group that regularly experiences extreme states of mind together. It can also be addictive, which may indicate unresolved psychological issues.

One should also be careful when considering the group leader. Be wary of psychedelic or spiritual group leaders who exhibit the following behaviors:

Being territorial about their group members.

If a group leader questions a participant about what other groups they belong to or are considering joining, this is a red flag because that is none of their business. If the leader criticizes a participant for joining another group, this is even more concerning.

Being territorial about what type of psychedelics a participant uses outside the group.

If a group leader tries to deter you from using a psychedelic that you have access to from someone else or another group, reflect on the leader's intention. Is it right for them to control the substances you use? Is it possible they're trying to control you out of their insecurity? Why is it important for them to be your sole access to a psychedelic? Consider their unspoken motivation.

Placing special conditions on a participant's ability to attend the group.

If the leader tells a participant they need to decide if they are loyal to the leader or group before attending the next session, or that they should take a break to "think about it" before coming back, this is concerning. It's a form of psychological manipulation. It puts the participant in the position of inappropriate approval-seeking and surrendering their agency to someone else.

Advising a group member on whether they should cut off their relationships with family, friends, or other groups.

It should be alarming if the leader suggests ending one's relationship with a romantic partner or with one's family. This is especially true if they're not also a licensed therapist or counselor specializing in families and couples. This is textbook cult-like behavior.

     *   *   *

Although this may be obvious, it's best to prepare your substance yourself whether you're journeying alone or in a group. If someone prepares yours for you, and if they do it privately, you have no control over or knowledge of exactly what they put in your cup to drink.

You should require full disclosure about what you'll consume when someone prepares it for you.

If the leader is unwilling to disclose their formula, ask yourself why. Is it about power? Fostering dependency? Something else?

     *   *   *

Being in an optimal mindset (set) and environment (setting) are the main qualities for a safe and productive journey.

The meditations in the online program comprise a complete path even without the use of psychedelics. But for those who intend to go on a journey while practicing the techniques for a significant period or afterward, they serve two purposes.

I discussed the first purpose in the chapter, *My Experience,* in Part One. Meditation can prime one's mind to fully reveal profound spiritual insights during the journey. Certainly, meditation can prompt revelations to some degree without the use of substances. But in my experience, it doesn't come close to what's possible with psilocybin, LSD, or DMT.[22]

---

[22] I understand this may not be other people's experience with substance-free meditation. But I question a person's opinion that meditation can be as revelatory as psychedelics if that person has not experienced a psychedelic

The second purpose the meditations serve is to generally strengthen the mind and prepare it for the implicit challenges of journeying. This is discussed in the earlier chapter, *Meditation as a Protective Measure*, also in Part One.

Preparation also involves details including the following:

- scheduling
- deciding who to notify
- assessing your physical fitness and asking your doctor
- preparing your outer life
- watching videos to build your confidence
- reconsidering your dose and preparing for nausea

Those details and more are covered in the next chapter. After that, the chapter *Your Journey* will prepare you by describing a typical journey and recommending a couple different ways to approach yours.

The last two chapters in Part Two will discuss how to integrate your experience afterward and how to journey with a sitter if that's your preference. This is also worthwhile should you ever have a friend ask you to sit for them. Having a friend with whom you can trade sitting sessions with can be richly rewarding.

---

journey themself. If they have no basis for comparison, they can only rely on their bias, one rooted in religious tenets and personal inhibitions.

PREPARATION

You have the greatest leverage over the quality of your journey before the journey begins, during the preparation period.

Everything you do in the months, weeks, and days before your first sip of mushroom tea sets the momentum and direction of your trip. If you've done an excellent job preparing, you'll be able to relax and allow the experience to unfold of its own accord, without any worry.

SEVENTY-FOUR WEEKS BEFORE:

Establish a steady meditation practice.

Ideally, you'll meditate daily or at least four to five times per week. If you use the guided meditations from *The Path of the Golden Teacher* online program, most sessions will be forty-five minutes long.

If you choose to follow the suggested progression from Part One, you will practice the meditations for at least

Preparation

seventy-four weeks (around a year and a half) before journeying. It may seem like a long time to wait, but I believe doing it this way will yield a much more profound spiritual experience during your psychedelic journey than only going part-way will. **But there are no rules here, only recommendations.**

Time may be of the essence for you, for example, if you have a potentially terminal illness. In that case, I recommend you look through the list of meditations in Part One and create a shortened order of progression for yourself.

For example, you might spend some time on the Foundational series, and then practice the Heart series, then have your psychedelic journey. It's a much shorter progression, but better than not meditating at all.

Or you might choose to do six months of meditation in the order recommended in Part One, finishing the Heart series, then have a journey. After the journey, you would continue moving through the progression and have another journey several months later after completing the Space and Energy series, and so on.

No matter how much time you devote to meditation before your journey, it will support you. Meditation makes us intimately familiar with our inner landscape and teaches us to manage our state of mind. It reveals normally invisible aspects of our psychological and perceptual processes.

Simply put, meditation makes us more stable.

TWO MONTHS BEFORE:

Schedule your journey.

Pick the date for your journey and put it in your calendar. Choosing a date will affect your mind and daily choices between the day you schedule it and when it happens. Everything that happens will be viewed in the context of the lead-up to your journey. It can cause you to be especially careful how you treat yourself and others. It will also encourage you to consolidate and clarify your intentions.

Ideally, you'll be able to sandwich your journey between two days off work. The day before can be a time to relax and clear your mind with or without meditation.

It's also an excellent opportunity to determine whether you should follow through or cancel your journey.

Feeling anxious, fearful, worried, or insecure the day before your journey are sure indicators that you're not ready for it. Pushing through those feelings and doing it anyway will most likely result in an undesirable experience.

How many people have forced themselves to go on a journey regardless of the red flags because they spent hundreds or thousands of non-refundable dollars for the experience? That kind of pressure is unfortunate, and unnecessary.

The wonderful advantage of your situation is that you won't be losing money by deciding to postpone your experience. You have the advantage of flexibility, which allows you to be as careful as possible when deciding whether to go forward or pause. This isn't a race, so if tomorrow isn't the right day, the smartest and kindest decision you can make is to reschedule.

If you decide to move forward, taking the following day off work will give you time and space to reintegrate with the ordinary world and reflect on what happened during your experience.

Returning to the office, taking sales calls, and attending staff meetings the day immediately following a journey can be very uncomfortable and possibly unbearable. Not scheduling time off for the day after your journey is a wasted opportunity because you won't be able to comfortably absorb the spiritual and psychological insights you received.

Also, depending on your psychological makeup, your usual personal boundaries may be diminished, and your gregariousness amplified. Interrupting the Monday morning staff meeting to remind everyone that we're all one and we need to stop destroying the ecosystem while tearfully declaring your unconditional love for your coworkers may quite possibly be a career-limiting move.

If you have a therapist, let them know your plans.

If you regularly see a therapist, scheduling an appointment before and after your journey can also be supportive. They can notice a change in your personality, values, and priorities after your journey. But if you don't tell them you used psychedelics, it could be confusing to them and to the therapeutic process in general.

Not everybody shares everything with their therapist, though. So, like everything else in this book, this is only a recommendation.

Get some exercise and see your doctor.

If you get winded climbing up a flight of stairs, it's time to begin a gentle exercise regimen and/or visit your doctor.

One of the contraindications for taking a large dose of psilocybin is high blood pressure or other cardiovascular issues. Psilocybin can increase your blood pressure and your heart rate during a journey. If you're healthy but never exercise and lead a sedentary lifestyle, this could make you quite uncomfortable during your journey. It could also risk your life.

So, if you're healthy enough to do so, why not take a long walk several times a week at least and get your heart pumping more often? This or other forms of exercise will go a long way to preparing you for the physiological effects of using a psychedelic.

But if you're not sure whether you're healthy enough to or are incapable of walking longer than several minutes without feeling out of breath and needing to sit down, you should definitely consult your physician first.

ONE MONTH BEFORE:

Pacify your life.

This is a great time to maintain peaceful relationships with friends and family and to avoid turmoil and drama. If you're in the process of looking for a new job, moving to another home or city, involved in legal proceedings, or grieving a major personal loss, it may be best to wait until your life is more settled.

Psilocybin is an amplifier, not a silver bullet. It won't make you feel better if you're not already in a positive state of mind beforehand. It's likely to only intensify negative feelings. Of course, I'm not saying you should be in a perfect state of mind. But taking a large dose of psilocybin while you're in crisis is a bad idea.

Watch confidence-building videos.

Educational and inspiring videos will help you build confidence and feel positive anticipation for your upcoming journey. Here are some recommendations:

- Big Think (Dec. 2, 2022). *The real risks of psychedelics, explained by an expert | Dr. Matthew Johnson* – on YouTube

Preparation

- *Dosed* – at www.DosedMovie.com

- *Dosed: Trip of a Lifetime* – at www.DosedMovie.com

- *How to Change Your Mind* – on Netflix

- *Fantastic Fungi* – on Netflix

- Harvard Divinity School (Sept. 19, 2020). *Psilocybin & Mystical Experience: Implications for Healthy Psychological Functioning & Spirituality* – on YouTube

- *The Goop Lab with Gwyneth Paltrow: The Healing Trip* (the first episode of the series) – on Netflix

- *Have a Good Trip: Adventures in Psychedelics* - on Netflix

- *The Last Shaman* (Even though this is about ayahuasca, it's still pertinent to the psycho-spiritual drive and use of psychedelic medicine.) – on Amazon Prime

- Kristy Arnett Moreno (Feb. 12, 2021). *My husband tried Mushroom Therapy. I thought he went crazy.* – on YouTube

- SXSW (Apr. 12, 2023). *How Psilocybin Mushrooms Can Help Save the World, with Paul Stamets* – on YouTube

Prime your mind with nature.

Visiting your local zoo or aquarium will fill your mind with beautiful representations of life and nature. Pay special attention to their visual patterns such as the zebra's stripes, the anaconda's scales, and the flowing tentacles of the jellyfish.

Making prolonged eye contact with primates like gorillas and orangutans can produce new and meaningful connections.

It's quite possible that one of the animals you connect with will reappear in your mind's eye during your psychedelic journey, perhaps bringing a special message.

If you dislike zoos, then choose an acceptable alternative such as visiting the botanic garden or your local park, going on a sunset hike, or strolling on the beach.

Stargazing on a warm, clear night can also be impactful, as can watching a show about the cosmos at the planetarium.

ONE WEEK BEFORE:

Pause your microdosing regimen.

If you've been microdosing, stop at least one week prior. Stopping ahead of time will eliminate any tolerance your body may have developed toward psilocybin. This will allow your journey dose to take full effect.

If microdosing has helped you with issues related to anxiety or stress, it will be important to replace it with supportive choices and activities this week. Avoid social media and television. Instead, exercise, spend time outside, engage in your favorite hobbies, and spend extra time with positive friends and relatives.

Preparation

Re-read the following chapters in this book.

- *How to Determine Your Ideal Journey Dose*
- *How to Consume Your Journey Dose*
- *Boosting Your Journey*

Prepare your audio playlist.

Prepare a long playlist to be accessible on your mobile device. It should be something without commercial interruptions. It can be quite irritating when the ambient track on your YouTube playlist is interrupted by car insurance commercials every five minutes. Taking off your mask to look at your screen to find the "skip" button on the YouTube app is also annoying. So, choose an app that provides commercial-free music.

I recommend ambient music without words. I prefer music with natural harmonics such as indigenous flutes and didgeridoos. I also enjoy electronic music. There are also well-known online playlists for psychedelic journeys that utilize Western classical music, which uses artificial harmonics. The most important thing is for you to choose the music you enjoy.

Avoid emotionally provocative music and select something relaxing or that provokes a sense of curiosity and wonder instead. You want your heart's expression to be spontaneous and genuine, not dictated by the music.

Your journey will likely last anywhere from three to six hours. Think about whether you'd like to replay a two-hour playlist three times, or a three-hour playlist twice, or prepare a single, six-hour playlist.

As a precaution, you might prepare a separate playlist comprised of music you know has a mood-lifting quality for you. This is a playlist you can play if your emotional state darkens, and you want to lift yourself out of it. Switching to something that makes you happy is a simple and effective way to brighten things up.

Some journeyers will choose to explore their darker emotions, but in any case, it's always nice to have this option when they reach their limit and would like to change direction.

Listening to a drumming track at the start of your journey can help provoke the visual hallucinations. Humans on every continent have probably been drumming ever since they started skinning animals for clothing.

Listening to or playing drums are not by themselves acts of cultural appropriation, so you don't have to worry about that, unless you're being culturally appropriative, of course. Cultural appropriation occurs when a dominant culture inappropriately adopts cultural elements from a minority culture. Just be yourself, there's no need to pretend to be from another culture. You are enough.

Not all drumming tracks are the same, so avoid making a last-minute random selection during your journey. Listen to several ahead of time to choose the one that feels most right to you.

Drum Track Download:

I created a 20-minute drumming track specifically for use during the start of a journey. It's available to download for free at:

www.WisdomWithin.space/PathOfTheGoldenTeacher

Preparation

Consolidate your intentions for your journey.

If you've engaged in a spiritual discipline such as meditation, chances are you already have a general intention for your journey. Your spiritual path may be predicated on prior events like personal inquiry, trauma, or existential crisis. In that case, you might use the journey as an adjunct to your contemplative practice for addressing those events.

Similarly, there may be one or more questions you've been exploring in therapy for weeks, months, or longer. These questions can also be the seeds of your intention for your journey.

Or you might seek a direct experience that confirms and strengthens your religious faith.

It can be helpful to write down your reason for this journey. This way, you'll be able to review your intention every day leading up to it. This is a way of priming your mind to shape the experience in a meaningful way.

Your intention can be broad or specific, as long as it's genuine. The least helpful approach is to have no intention at all. That would be like sailing a boat without a rudder.

Schedule a check-in & check-out with a friend.

If you choose not to have a sitter with you, it can be a good idea to schedule a phone call with a trusted friend before and after your journey. You might also ask them to be available for phone calls during your journey in case you need them.

During your check-in, share your intentions. Sharing your intentions with another person naturally galvanizes them in your mind. If your friend is an experienced journeyer, they might offer you some helpful tips to help you prepare.

Schedule your check-out call for the evening of the date of your journey. Your friend will be wondering how it went and it would be better for them to hear everything's fine sooner than later.

If you don't feel like talking to anyone that evening, send your friend a text message letting them know you're fine and that you'll call them the next day instead.

Give your friend your emergency contact information.

As safe as psychedelics like psilocybin are, there are always risks, and there's no benefit to pretending there aren't. Because of that, give your friend (the one you'll have a check-in call with) your emergency contact information. Make it clear that they have your full permission to call your emergency contact should anything happen, such as a visit to the hospital.

The statistical probability that something this severe will occur is minuscule. But it can help you and your friend relax during the journey just by them knowing who to call if extra support is needed.

Go food shopping.

Make sure you have all the food you'll need for the day of your journey. Ideally, you won't need to leave home that morning to do any last-minute shopping. And you should not drive at all after your journey until the next day.

Preparation

ON THE DAY OF YOUR JOURNEY:

No driving today.

You must commit to not driving a vehicle at any point after you consume your psychedelic until the following morning.

After several hours, you may feel that your trip is finished and you're clear-headed. But driving a car demands vigilance, normal reaction time, focus, and the ability to process the speeds of other cars.

You might feel sober while sitting in your living room. But if you make the bad decision to get in your car and enter traffic, you'll realize you're not quite back to normal yet. You'll find yourself in a difficult and potentially deadly situation.

If you need company, ask your friends to come over. If you truly need to get out of the house, ask a friend to drive you.

But hopefully, your kitchen is stocked with your favorite foods. Why not make some popcorn and enjoy a nice movie before going to bed? Or read a book. Or do some art. Play your guitar.

Do anything, *anything*, to keep yourself from getting in the car that day. Think of the potential consequences should you be pulled over: losing your license, time in court, thousands of dollars in fees, and many months of mandatory DUI classes every weekend.

Eat a light meal one or two hours before.

If you'd like to journey in the morning, plan to have a light breakfast at least an hour or two before. Or if journeying in the mid-afternoon, enjoy a light lunch, also waiting an hour or two for your stomach to empty its contents into the lower digestive tract.

An empty stomach will reduce the chance of nausea and its severity after drinking your mushroom tea[23] or eating your mushrooms whole.

Prepare your room.

Whether it's your bedroom, living room, or a secluded cabin, your room will serve as a sacred space for your journey. What "sacred" means is up to you. "Special" is another great word because it's nice for the environment to represent the intention and we want this to be a very special experience.

On one hand, it doesn't matter what your room looks like because you'll have a blindfold on most of the time. Journeying can resemble being inside a movie theater. We tend to become so absorbed in the film that we completely forget that we're in a room filled with rows of seats occupied by dozens of strangers.

On the other hand, making the effort to prepare your room serves to concretize your intention for journeying. You have a specific reason for doing this. Cleaning and decorating your space serve as psychological preparation for achieving your purpose.

You might hang special artwork on your walls or place religious or spiritual objects on your nightstand along with framed pictures of your ancestors, immediate family, friends, and spiritual mentors.

Have your check-in call with your friend.

At some point in the morning, have your check-in call with your friend. Confirm that you're about to begin and review your intentions for the journey. Together, decide on

---

[23] See Part Three for how to consume your mushrooms.

Preparation

what time you'll call later that afternoon or evening to let them know you're alright. Don't leave them wondering or they'll be worried!

If in doubt, postpone.

Before starting your journey, you should carefully examine your state of mind. You can do this during your check-in call with a friend, or any point before you consume your journey dose. Keep in mind that psilocybin is an **amplifier**, so whatever you feel now is likely to be intensified after taking your dose.

To be clear, if you feel anxious before taking your dose, you should **not** expect the psilocybin to relax you. Expect the opposite. You're more likely to become extremely anxious after the psilocybin kicks in. This would certainly lead to a challenging journey.

Therefore, it is important for you to either find a way to reduce the anxiety before taking your dose or postpone your journey for another day after you've prepared yourself better.

It should also be said that a small amount of nervousness is normal, especially if it's your first time. But if you also feel optimistic, are well-prepared, curious, confident, and in a good mood, this will go a long way to counteracting the nervousness and leading your journey in a positive direction.

Prepare for nausea.

Mushrooms contain a polysaccharide called *chitin* (pronounced "kite-n") which can be irritating to the stomach. Chitin is normally broken down during the cooking process. But in our case, our psilocybin mushrooms have only been dried, not cooked.

People with very sensitive stomachs can have a bowel movement or even vomit after consuming psilocybin mushrooms. But these experiences should not be compared to the "purge" that can accompany the use of ayahuasca.

Most commonly, users will experience light-to-moderate nausea which will lessen throughout the journey. In my experience, the nausea is usually converted to uniquely pleasurable sensations in the abdomen.

Still, it can be worthwhile to mitigate the nausea if possible. Ginger is a well-known nausea reducer. That's why I typically mix ginger tea with hot chocolate for the base of my psilocybin brew.

Ginger also comes in the form of chewy candy or gummies. There are various brands of ginger chews available in pharmacies and grocery stores specifically for morning sickness and pre-natal relief.

Cannabis can also reduce nausea when used before taking psilocybin. This is discussed in greater detail in the chapter *Cannabis with Meditation and Psilocybin* in Part Four.

However, using two mind-altering substances at the same time is not recommended for beginners. So, if it's your first time using psilocybin, consider skipping the cannabis and relying on ginger. And wait at least an hour or two after eating a meal before drinking your psilocybin tea.

Another option is to use "lemon tek," the technique of mixing your mushroom powder with lemon juice. The juice's acid can help break down the chitin, making it easier for your stomach to digest.

Just pour your mushroom powder into a shot glass or similar and add one to two ounces of lemon juice (not to be confused with lemonade). Mix them and let them sit for a couple of minutes before downing the brew.

If you have digestive issues or are sensitive to acidic foods or bitter flavors, it might be best to avoid this method.

Preparation

Lemon-tekkers typically report a rapid onset or "come-up" of the psychedelic effects but with a shorter overall duration of the journey.

Reconsider your dose.

Re-read the chapter *How to Determine Your Ideal Journey Dose* in Part Three. Then, weigh your levels of confidence, optimism, and relaxation against your levels of fear, hesitation, and anxiety to help decide how much to take.

For example, look at the chart in that chapter. If your ideal microdose is 0.1 grams, then an appropriate journey dose could be anywhere from half a gram to one gram assuming the psilocybin is highly potent[24].

So, if you're feeling more on the cautious side, take something around half a gram. If you're feeling perfectly comfortable and ready, you might consider a full gram, something in between, or even more than a gram.

If it's your first time, please remember there'll be opportunities for journeys with larger doses down the road with the benefit of prior experience. There's no need to take an unnecessarily large dose now.

Commit to staying off the phone and internet until your journey is complete.

If there are any phone calls you need to make, or any web surfing you want to do, do them before starting your journey and commit to staying offline until you're sure your trip is over.

It's possible to feel a sense of grandiosity during a journey. You might have insights that you'd like to share "Right now!" in the middle of your experience.

---

[24] See the chapter *How to Test for Potency*.

Perhaps you want to apologize to one of your children for something you did ten years ago. Or you want to call your mentor and let them know how grateful you are for their support and wisdom. Or you want to tell your ex-spouse exactly what you think of them and why you're doing so much better without them in your life.

Calling that person while under the influence of psilocybin could be hilarious in the least, and disastrous in the worst. Remember that you'll be in an extremely altered state of mind, and it will be obvious to the person on the other end of the line.

This may cause them to become concerned about your mental health, especially if you haven't told them you're under the mushroom's influence. If you don't want certain people to know you use psilocybin, calling them during a journey is the fastest way for you to violate your own privacy.

The same considerations apply to using social media. You might believe you're posting invaluable pearls of wisdom or nuggets of comedic gold on your profile for everyone to see. But you might embarrass yourself and tarnish your professional reputation and public image instead.

So, make the firm decision to *not* call anyone and *not* to get on the internet until your journey is over and you're stone-cold sober.

The exception would be if you need to call the police, paramedics, or other health and safety professionals because you're in physical danger or are experiencing a psychological crisis such as suicidality.[25]

---

[25] If you're in the United States and are having thoughts of suicide, please call or text 988 for help or visit https://988lifeline.org. If you're outside the U.S., please look up your local suicide prevention services and make sure you know how to reach them during your journey if necessary. If you're at risk of suicide, DO NOT USE PSYCHEDELICS. **Remember that the use of psychedelics is *contraindicated* for those with suicidal ideation.**

YOUR JOURNEY

No two journeys are alike. Still, it can be helpful for first-timers to be oriented to the experience ahead of time. It is impossible to note every single aspect that may arise for the journeyer, but hopefully, this description will be enough to help you remain at ease and feel prepared for each stage of the experience.

Before consuming your psilocybin tea[26], make sure your environment (bedroom, living room couch, etc.) is prepared, your playlist is ready, and your blindfold is within reach. If you'll be on the living room couch, make sure extra blankets and pillows are available.

Now comes the time to drink the tea, assuming you feel confident about moving forward. Remember that feeling a little bit nervous is fine, but feeling significant anxiety can

---

[26] This description assumes you'll be using psilocybin. The overall description is similar to that of LSD, although LSD trips can last twice as long, if not longer, depending on dosage. As for a description of a DMT journey, see the chapter *How to Use DMT*.

Path of the Golden Teacher

lead to a challenging experience and is a signal to postpone until another day when you feel more settled and optimistic.

It's best to drink it all within several minutes instead of spreading it out over an hour. You'll want to be able to evaluate the full effect of the dose an hour later to decide whether to use a booster dose[27].

It can take anywhere from twenty minutes to a full hour before feeling the onset. While you wait, it's a good idea to review your intentions for your journey. If you're by yourself, re-read them if you've written them down ahead of time. If you have a sitter, this is a great time to share your intention with them, even if you already have before.

This is also a good time to meditate. Rather than use a technique, simply sit still and notice the subtle sensations in your body and mind. I enjoy playing rhythmic, overtone-producing instruments like the jaw harp[28], frame drum, and didgeridoo. Instruments like these can enhance relaxation and induce trance-like states.

At this stage, psilocybin, psilocyn, baeocystin, norbaeocystin, aeruginascin, and other compounds are being processed by your digestive system and liver and making their way to your brain.

The first significant sensation you might feel is nausea due to the chitin from the mushroom. It can help to note the sensation and how it changes over time. As the psychedelic effect becomes stronger, the nausea can convert into more of a soft and squishy sensation in your belly, even a pleasurable one.

Around the same time or soon after, you'll feel slightly different, or "off." This is like having had several sips of wine

---

[27] See the chapter *Boosting Your Journey*.

[28] Like the drum, jaw harps have been used across the globe for millennia. They have been used by shamans as well as folk musicians. To watch videos about different types of jaw harps and order your own, visit www.TheHarpery.com

Your Journey

or liquor and feeling the buzz. When this feeling arrives, it's time to head to your journey space, get comfortable, start your playlist, and put on your blindfold.

The slightly "off" feeling can evolve into slight trembling, chills, or other flu-like sensations. These are normal and should not be a cause for concern. I regularly experience ringing in the ear (tinnitus) and it usually worsens during the onset of my trips. And at some point, it returns to normal.

These types of physical sensations are referred to as "body load." Psychedelics are taxing on the body, so the more accustomed to physical stress you are, for example through regular exercise, the better.

Learning about these possibilities now should go a long way to helping you stay calm when those sensations arise for you.

In time, visual hallucinations will appear. You can help this process by actively looking not with your eyes, but with your attention. You can do this by pretending to see through your blindfold as if to see something "out there." You can also turn your attention within and focus on the imaginal space of mind, the place you go when you daydream.

Over the next couple of hours, the hallucinations will increase, peak, then slowly come to an end. They can appear as ever-changing geometric puzzles, natural landscapes, an urban skyline replete with tall buildings, or futuristic scenes. In your mind's eye, the colors can appear in muted pastels, vivid neon, glimmering mother-of-pearl, and more.

People with color blindness should pay careful attention to what appears during their journey because they might experience colors differently than usual.

You might witness real and mythological animals. I've seen anacondas, primates, and twenty-foot-tall tarantulas. I've also seen emerald dragons and rainbow unicorns. I'm not joking. One of the unicorns had two horns, so I suppose that would make it a super-tall rainbow goat instead.

If you notice animals, mysterious figures, aliens, disembodied eyes, or other beings looking at you, don't assume they have negative intentions. The first time I saw a dragon, I became afraid but quickly realized it had no interest in harming me. After waiting several moments, I realized its intentions were benevolent. It was just hard to tell because reptiles don't make facial expressions the way primates do.

It's best to remember these creatures originate in your brain. They *are* you. Yes, they can frighten you the same way you become frightened during a nightmare. But when you realize you're having a nightmare and it's not "real," the fear quickly recedes. So, if you get scared, try to remember it's just a hallucination, it's your own mind, and it'll soon pass.

Whatever visions you see, you may notice they are influenced by your playlist, at least to some degree. So, if at any point you really need to improve your experience, feel free to change your music selection. You can also take a break from the visions by removing your blindfold and looking around the room. You'll notice the hallucinations have stopped and you're safely in bed or on the couch.

If you notice your clock while changing your playlist, you'll realize your sense of time is greatly diminished. You might feel as if three hours have passed only to realize you're only one and a half hours in. Or you might feel like you've been journeying for one hour but two have already passed. At any point in the experience, it's possible to become so absorbed in it that you even forget that you're journeying. You're just *in it*.

Within an hour or two, your nausea is likely to have abated.

Just like in regular life, you will eventually need to relieve yourself. As you stand up, your legs may feel a little shaky and your balance wobbly. For safety, never walk anywhere while wearing your blindfold. Don't worry about ruining the experience by interrupting it with a bathroom

Your Journey

break. As soon as you return and put the blindfold back on, you'll quickly return to the hallucinatory state.

While in the bathroom, why not take the opportunity to look at yourself in the mirror? You might notice the colors in the room have shifted slightly. And your face may appear different. What is it like to look into your own eyes?

The usual filters with which you judge your appearance may be offline, and now you can appreciate yourself without that conditioning. This is a great opportunity to feel love and appreciation for the true "you" without those filters. You might also realize something about the filters you apply to other people every day.

Eventually, the journey will enter a more meaningful phase. You might become aware of knowledge and insights you've never considered before. These could be related to family, friends, spirituality, physics, our ecosystem, galaxy, or the entire universe.

It's possible to suddenly perceive yourself from inside your own body, such as in your intestines, brain, or reproductive organs. Your body may be communicating warnings, comments about your habits or diet, or assurances that everything is just as it's supposed to be, and you can stop worrying.

A certain person from your past might show up. This could be someone you feel unexpressed gratitude for. Or it could be someone who severely hurt you, and with whom you need closure.

It might also be a deceased pet, relative, or spiritual guide.

And it can even be more than that, like feeling as if you've become one with Source, God, Allah, Yahweh, Vajradhara, universal consciousness, or whatever spiritual label you use for the ultimate basis of reality. That level of experience is beyond words, and you must experience it to know it.

Depending on what arises, you may feel intense emotions. These can range from laughing uproariously, weeping inconsolably, screaming with rage, or trembling with fear. The chapter *Meditation as a Protective Measure* in Part One explains how meditation increases your capacity to allow and be present in these experiences.

It's also possible to feel degrees of love you've never felt before. Many people rate their psychedelic experience as being in the top five events of their lives. Once, a friend of mine rated her first journey as better than the birth of her child.

After feeling your heart opening, you might suddenly desire human contact. If you choose to use a sitter and that person is your spouse, partner, or trusted friend, this will be fortunate. These are safe people to receive a hug from or to hold hands with. Theirs are good shoulders to cry on.

If you journey alone, you'll need to wait until sometime after your journey to find someone to connect with. But being alone can reduce the craving for human contact since you'll already know it's not immediately available.

It's also possible to fear that you've permanently lost your mind. It's an intense degree of paranoia and is *less* likely to occur to those who know what to expect ahead of time. The psychedelic journey *is* a temporary deviation from regular brain function, and you will not feel like your normal self for several hours.

But it *is* temporary, assuming you do not have a history of a psychotic disorder or are at risk of having one.[29] If you do, then don't use psychedelics.

No matter what visions, insights, and emotions come, they'll eventually wane. This period can take an hour or two before you feel completely back to normal.

---

[29] See the chapter *Contraindications for Psychedelics* here in Part Two.

Your Journey

But what is normal? Yes, you'll be sober, but you'll be profoundly changed by what happened. Integrating those changes will be discussed in the next chapter.

The rest of the day should be spent at home (or wherever you had your journey). Engage in relaxing or contemplative activities or take a stroll outside. Watching an epic saga on TV while enjoying a delicious dinner can be nice too.

Since this book concerns meditation, we should discuss two different approaches to journeying before concluding this chapter.

The first approach is to simply recline in bed or on the couch and let the experience unfold organically.

The second approach is to practice sitting meditation during the journey. Since the experience can last several hours, it's more practical to alternate sitting with lying down.

As mentioned earlier, you could meditate immediately after drinking your brew while carefully noting perceptual changes and new sensations. Beyond that, follow your instinct about when and how much to sit up during your journey.

If your intention for journeying involves an illness, injury, or questions about your body, you could meditate to scan your body or send love and healing energy to whatever parts need it the most. With the aid of the psychedelic, this could be a rich and colorful experience.

If you practice meditative techniques involving subtle-body visualization (channels, chakras, seeing yourself as a representational deity, etc.), this is a great opportunity to experience them in new ways.

While sitting upright during a recent journey, I felt compelled to turn my head to the left as far as it could go while twisting my torso and arms. I must have held that posture for twenty minutes because it felt so good. I can't say for sure why my body asked for this. Maybe it was simply to get a good stretch in. Or maybe it involved unwinding and releasing subtle energy that had become stuck somehow.

Path of the Golden Teacher

I don't need to know, though. What was important was that I paid attention to what my body asked for, I followed its direction, and it felt wonderful.

Body load, the bodily stress from taking a psychedelic, can make it difficult to sit up for extended periods without physical support. Of course, this depends on dosage. But you can expect to tire after sitting upright for some time.

Instead of sitting the way you normally do, it might be enough to sit up in bed and lean back on the headboard. Or if you've been lying on the couch, just sit up and lean back.

It's important not to put unrealistic expectations on yourself. Doing so can diminish your journey, possibly robbing yourself of rich experiences. If it's your first time journeying, I recommend forgoing any plans to practice sitting meditation during your journey. Just lie down and relax.

Those who practice yoga *asanas* (postures) will be familiar with *savasana*, the corpse pose. This is often done at the end of a yoga session to passively integrate the experience into one's being.

Journeying done entirely lying down can be regarded as a special type of savasana.

It might be interesting to explore easy asanas like child's pose, cat-cow pose, or a gentle cobra pose. Caution is necessary with these or any other poses, though.

Psychedelics alter your bodily perception and can dull the experience of pain. Therefore, it's possible to over-stretch your muscles, ligaments, and joints without knowing it, only to feel the pain after the psychedelic has worn off.

This also applies to those who use cannabis during their journey to control nausea or other reasons because it is an effective pain killer.

If you're a practitioner of the *Path of the Golden Teacher* online program and have at least completed the minimum recommended session, then I suggest you lie down, relax, and let the journey unfold organically. You've done the preliminary work, now it's time to let go and reap the rewards.

INTEGRATION

People often associate integration with sharing your psychedelic experience with a sitter, a therapist, a shaman, or a group of other journeyers. In this case, the other person serves as a mirror reflecting your newfound insights to you. But if you prefer to integrate your experience by yourself, that works just as well.

Integration doesn't have to be complicated. Essentially, it's the opportunity for you to reflect on what happened to you on emotional, cognitive, and physical levels during your journey. And the most important aspect is time. Your brain just went through a major disruption in its usual mode of functioning and needs *time* for two things to happen, rest and reorganization.

Ideally, you will have scheduled the day after your journey as a day to yourself. Returning to your job or other responsibilities robs you of time to contemplate and absorb the many a-ha moments you had. It can be a missed opportunity. But if you can't have a day dedicated to integration after the journey, don't worry, because integration isn't a one-day affair. Integration can take weeks or months, if not the rest of one's life.

If your journey brings up previously unexpressed sadness or other emotions related to the death of a loved one, integration may serve as initiating a period of grief which can be healing. There is no standard formula or duration for grief. Everyone does it differently. But having the space and time to recognize, "Yes, this must be what grief is. I'm grieving." is crucial to fruitfully engaging the grief.

Grief isn't reserved for the death of loved ones. Grief comes with many forms of loss such as a breakup, divorce, unemployment, loss of physical or mental abilities due to accident, illness, or age, or surviving physical, sexual, or emotional abuse.

Journeys can reveal new and profound spiritual insights. They can differ from what you have been taught by your religion of birth, your parents, or your social circle. For some people, this is a time of celebration because it grants them the freedom and courage to follow a new path, unique to them.

For others, the new insights can be extremely challenging because the person would prefer to maintain their current worldview.

They don't enjoy having their belief system challenged, especially by their own mind. Nobody likes being challenged by others or by their own self. Cognitive dissonance, holding two views that contradict each other, is stressful especially when it concerns our core values and beliefs.

For these people, integration is a time for them to contemplate new ideas and choose what to make of them. And it is a choice. Just because you received an insight or experienced a new point of view during a journey *doesn't automatically make it true.*

Nobody should surrender their personal authority to the psychedelic experience.

Integration

Every day, we're exposed to new ideas in person and through the internet. We're well-practiced at filtering those ideas and deciding what to accept and reject. Just because an idea came to you during a journey doesn't grant it immunity from your cognitive filtration system. It's perfectly alright to reject or remain undecided about the information you received during the journey.

Sometimes the easiest response is to say to yourself, "Hmm, that was interesting. I'll think about it, but I'm not in any hurry. For now, I'm still happy with my current belief system and don't see a need to change it."

It's also important to *not* make a major life change immediately after your journey. You might have developed the idea that your spouse doesn't love you and it's time for a divorce. Or that you're deeply unhappy at your job and you need to quit as soon as the office opens on Monday.

Or that it's about time you visited your ancestral homeland on the other side of the planet. And even though you can't afford it, it's suddenly so important you'll just have to charge it to your credit card.

Since you're quitting your job anyway, why not book a flight next week, right? Wrong.

Consider making it your policy to not make any major life changes for at least several months after your journey. You may have metabolized the psychedelic in one day, but that doesn't mean you're completely back to normal afterward. It's normal to feel profound levels of inspiration and renewed purpose for days if not weeks or longer after a journey.

But those feelings will wane after a while, and at that point, you'll be left with the consequences of actions you took during the afterglow.

You might realize that couple counseling is the next step, not asking for divorce. And that you can apply for new jobs while staying at your current one to maintain a steady income while you look. And that you can wait to take that trip-of-a-lifetime for when you've accrued enough paid vacation time. That place isn't going anywhere, so there's no need to rush.

It just so happens that the same challenges and considerations apply to meditation retreats lasting one or more weeks. Endless hours of rumination, concentration, and plain old daydreaming on the meditation cushion can cause the person to think it's time to make a big change.

But just like the psychedelic journeyer, the meditator on retreat is not in a normal state of mind and should wait before taking action. All the principles of integration described in this chapter are equally applicable after a meditation retreat.

As for what to do while integrating on the day after a journey, low-key activities like journaling, walking in nature, or lazing around the house are great options.

If you followed the recommendations in the chapter *Preparation*, you will have scheduled a phone call with a trusted friend to follow up with them and let them know you're doing okay. Sharing your insights and questions during the call or visit will support your integration process. Practicing *integration meditation* (from Part One) can also be helpful that day.

HOW TO JOURNEY WITH A SITTER

Choosing Your Sitter

If you would like to have a trusted friend with you during your journey, ask them to be part of your process early enough so they can reserve the day in their calendar.

Apart from ensuring their availability, giving them advance notice will help them feel like an integral part of your process, which both of you will appreciate. Sitting for each other has the potential to strengthen and deepen your friendship.

You might also schedule a phone call or visit with your sitter the day before and after your journey.

The day before, share your intention for journeying with them. Their role is simply to be a mirror for you. Stating your intentions to another person has a concretizing effect on your consciousness. It also gives your sitter a basis for asking, "So, did you fulfill your intention?" afterward, as a point for review.

Your sitter is your witness. Before your journey, they'll observe your state of mind and acknowledge the steps you've taken to prepare yourself. They should also acknowledge your courageous decision to move forward. It's normal to have a small degree of trepidation ahead of a journey. But if your sitter notices a concerning amount, they must call attention to it and suggest you postpone it.

You should feel no need to impress your sitter or prove anything to them. They should be prepared for a last-minute cancellation and be completely supportive of that decision.

If you and your friend have agreed to trade sitting for each other, you should honor your end of the bargain and sit for your friend even though you chose to cancel your journey. After all, they cleared their calendar that whole day to be with you.

When trading sitting services with a friend, the journeys should never be on the same day, or even the day after. If you journey first, you'll want to have the next day to yourself for relaxed integration. Consider trading over two weekends instead.

During your journey, your sitter may witness you crying profoundly, laughing uproariously, screaming angrily, or doing very little at all.

Though it's rare with psilocybin, you might experience incontinence or vomiting, and your sitter will be there to assist in those cases as well.

But this is about more than practical matters. During your session, you may feel a powerful drive to be seen, acknowledged, and witnessed by another human. This is inherent in humans. We know ourselves, in part, through the eyes of others. This is why isolation can lead to depression and other mental health concerns.

And though it's possible to achieve a *sense of meaning* while alone, meaning is greatly multiplied when shared between two or more people.

This is what makes the role of the sitter a sacred one. When the journeyer needs to feel seen or share their insights, the sitter is there to receive them. Apart from the psychedelic experience itself, that interaction between the journeyer and sitter is the first manifestation of meaning after the trip.

After your journey, your sitter might reflect how you've integrated any insights you received into your day-to-day life, helping you note the changes in your sense of self.

You should schedule another call or a visit with your sitter anytime later should you need additional support or feedback.

So, after reading the above, ask yourself, "Who do I trust enough to do this for me? Who will be respectful of me when I'm emotionally vulnerable or if I throw up? Who is stable and secure enough to listen to me cry for two hours straight without running out of the room? And who will keep everything that happened between us private?"

This should be a friend whom you have known for at least several years, someone with a dependable, respectful, and trustworthy character.

It should also be someone with whom there is no potential or unacknowledged sexual attraction. If you harbor secret feelings for them, you'll likely feel compelled to air those feelings and possibly make an inappropriate advance to your sitter.

The worst thing that could happen is for them to accept your invitation and take advantage of you while you're in an altered state.

With that type of person, the reverse is true too. They may confess their sexual attraction to you even without your prompting them and even if you are not attracted to them. Then, they may try to take advantage of you while you're under the influence regardless of your response.

The exception would be if your spouse or significant other is sitting for you, or you for them. If you have a healthy, well-established, long-term sexual relationship with them, that's different.

But still, you and your significant other should establish clear boundaries before either one of you goes under the influence. For one spouse to force the other to have sex especially when the one being forced is under the influence is still considered assault, an extreme violation with severe repercussions.

Boundaries and Agreements

Here is a list of items to agree on with your sitter well before your journey begins. Both parties need to be in complete agreement about each one. It is also highly recommended to write these agreements on paper and for both parties to sign and date them.

- Where will the sitter be physically located?

    Is the sitter to remain in the living room while the journeyer is in the bedroom, within earshot? Or is the sitter to be in a chair several feet away from the bed? Or other?

- What kind of physical contact is allowed?

    What happens if the journeyer is talking to the sitter and begins to cry? Is the sitter allowed to hold the journeyer's hand in support? Is hugging allowed at any point during the journey?
    If the two adults are married or in a mature, long-term romantic relationship, is sex allowed? Is that part of the journeyer's intention, to experience sex while tripping? Both people need to consent to sexual contact before one of them is under the influence.

How to Journey with a Sitter

- How, and how often, should the sitter check on the journeyer?

    Should the sitter simply remain in the other room the whole time unless the journeyer calls out to them? Or should the sitter quietly open the bedroom door and do a visual check every half-hour? If not every half-hour, then how often?
    If the journeyer doesn't respond to the sitter's entrance, should the sitter rouse the journeyer by tapping their shoulder or speaking loud enough to be heard over the music?
    How about using hand signals for brief check-ins, such as the sitter gesturing with a thumbs-up/thumbs-down motion, and the journeyer responding with a thumbs-up to indicate they're doing well and wish to be left alone to continue journeying without further interruption?
    If they're not doing so well, or if they'd like to chat with the sitter, then the journeyer should remove their blindfold and verbally communicate their wishes.

- Who controls the journeyer's phone and laptop?

    As mentioned in the chapter *Preparation*, it's possible to engage in poor decision-making while under the influence.
    Pronounced grandiosity combined with new insights about relationships or the state of the universe can compel a journeyer to pick up the phone and start calling. Or to log on to social media and start posting. This is a very bad idea.
    If your sitter notices you on the phone or laptop, do they have permission to question what you're doing? Do they have permission to take your devices away from you for your protection?

Or should you place your devices in your sitter's charge before you even begin your journey just to be safe?

As part of this agreement, it can be helpful for there to be a separate line item where the journeyer states their commitment to not call anyone or engage with social media or email for the duration of their journey.

- Who's in charge of preparing a booster dose if necessary? And how much psilocybin will be used?

    As you'll learn in the chapter *Boosting Your Journey* in Part Three, journeyers can take a booster dose around an hour after their first dose should the initial experience be too weak.

    Using a digital scale, weighing out psilocybin powder, and preparing the tea can be difficult tasks even with the effects of a moderate psilocybin dose.

    The journeyer might be tempted to make risky, last-minute adjustments to the dosage. So, agree ahead of time that the sitter will be responsible for weighing the powder and preparing the tea if a booster dose is warranted.

    Also agree on how much the dose will be (see the chapter *Boosting Your Journey* for recommendations), and that no last-minute increases will be permitted.

How to Journey with a Sitter

Good Communication During a Journey

The following tips are provided in the case that the sitter is not a licensed therapist or counselor.

Don't contradict the journeyer because you want to make them feel better.

For example, if the journeyer says, "I feel so ugly. My life's a total mess and nobody likes me," the sitter may be compelled to reply, "Oh honey, you're not ugly, you're beautiful, can't you see? Your life is fine, and plenty of people like you. I'm here for you, aren't I?"

The intention is good, but it won't work. Rereading the sitter's response, it's easy to see that they directly challenged the journeyer's viewpoint. It was a total shutdown and rejection of their experience.

Even though the journeyer may not consciously identify the shutdown, some part of them did feel the rejection. The risk is the journeyer may realize their feelings are not being respected or accepted. Their trust in the sitter will diminish and they might stop sharing altogether.

Try reflecting and saying "tell me more" instead.

Instead of trying to make your journeyer feel better, reflect what you heard back to them so they feel heard. For the example above, a simple response like, "You don't like the way you look. You feel rejected." can go a long way.

The journeyer will know that you were listening carefully, which implies respect. And they'll know you were listening without judging what they said.

It may seem counterintuitive, but challenging someone's negativity to make them feel better *is* a form of judgment. But listening and reflecting is non-judgmental and conveys acceptance.

After the sitter reflects what they heard, they should wait for the journeyer to respond. Even if the journeyer corrects the sitter's reflection, that's great. It's another opportunity for the sitter to listen and reflect more. It keeps the communication going.

If or when the journeyer stops responding, the sitter can say, "Tell me more." This lets the journeyer know the sitter is still available and willing to hear more from the other person.

If the journeyer is stuck in a thought loop, offer a course correction.

It's possible for a journeyer to get stuck in a thought loop when chatting with their sitter. What initially seemed like a brief sharing can become a half-hour series of repeated ideas with no sign of approaching resolution.

Time distortion is common with psychedelics, and the journeyer may not have noticed how much time has passed since the conversation began. They probably don't realize that their journey will be ending soon, and they may want to explore it more before that time comes.

The sitter can assist them by offering a course correction. It can be enough to say something like, "Hey friend, I notice that we've been talking about this for a long time now. Do you feel complete with this topic? You might only have one or two hours left. Would you like to go lie down again and re-enter your journey? Or would you like to continue talking about this? It's your choice, I just don't want you to miss out if you don't want to. I'm open to whatever you choose."

If the journeyer is having a challenging time, also offer a course correction.

Journeys can sometimes cause a person to feel afraid or confused. They might have remembered a past trauma or profound loss. They might be overwhelmed by the hyper-

How to Journey with a Sitter

geometric visuals. They might have dissociated from their body or from being human altogether and be experiencing existential dread. For one reason or another, they might be terrified they've lost their mind and want a way out, *now*.

The first thing the sitter can do is to remind the journeyer that they are under the influence. They might have forgotten that. Reminding them of the situation, and especially that everything will be back to normal in "a little while" (several hours or less) can bring immediate relief and even a little humor to the situation.

The sitter should offer to change the playlist to something with a happier or lighter tone. This simple act can positively alter the journey's trajectory.

Offering the journeyer fruit such as an orange or strawberries can redirect their mind via the senses. The smell, taste, and appearance of the fruit can be enough to pull them out of whatever dark hole they fell in.

If none of those work, the sitter could offer to take the journeyer outside, preferably in a backyard with privacy from the neighbors, for a stroll or to sit beneath a tree.

If the weather is cold, the sitter should ensure the journeyer is properly dressed to protect them from hypothermia.

Or put on a happy movie, cook some popcorn, order a pizza, or dish out some ice cream. Eating can feel grounding and even help the journey end sooner.

Bring out the warm blankets and teddy bears, and everything will feel better soon.

The journeyer should not take a bath or enter a hot tub while under the influence because of the risk of drowning or overheating. Showering poses a different risk. Overhead water spray can feel overwhelming like standing beneath a waterfall, heightening the journeyer's distress.

What does the sitter do the rest of the time?

If the journeyer is physically and psychologically well prepared for their journey, chances are that the sitter won't need to do anything. Their mere presence is enough for the journeyer to feel confident and more relaxed about what they're undertaking.

The sitter should plan on maintaining a quiet atmosphere. They should refrain from using headphones or listening to speakers because they need to hear any noises coming from the journeyer's room. Listening for silence, snoring, laughter, crying, or other sounds keeps the sitter informed of the journeyer's state of mind.

The sitter doesn't need to check on the journeyer every time they hear a new sound, but it's good to notice extreme shifts in the journeyer's state of mind. Most importantly, the sitter needs to listen for requests for assistance walking to the bathroom, getting a snack, or adjusting the thermostat.

Therefore, sitters should pass the time with silent activities like reading, yoga, making art, working on a puzzle, or catching up on emails.

Sitters should remember that the journeyer will be especially sensitive to their surroundings, including the sitter's mood. It's just as important for the sitter to be happy, calm, and confident as it is for the journeyer.

PART THREE

GROWING AND USING PSILOCYBIN

INTRODUCTION TO GROWING

Note: Specific, step-by-step instructions follow this introduction.

There are a variety of methods for growing psilocybin mushrooms at home. Here, you will learn the simplest method, using a pre-made grow bag. Other methods involve using canning jars, a pressure cooker, and large plastic storage tubs modified into *monotubs*.

These methods yield much larger quantities of mushrooms and are more satisfying for serious hobbyists and cultivators.

My book, *Blue Thumb: How to Grow Psilocybin Mushrooms at Home* (second edition), teaches three methods, including making your own grow bag from scratch instead of ordering a pre-made one online. The photos are in color, making it even more enjoyable.

When growing mushrooms, we simply mimic how they grow in nature. Spores, the reproductive cells, come together to become mycelium. In nature, mycelium grows as a network

Introduction to Growing

of delicate fibers underground. There, mycelium enjoys the darkness as well as the carbon dioxide, which it thrives on.

As the mycelium grows upward, reaching the surface of the ground, exposure to oxygen signals that it's time for the mycelium to produce its fruit, mushrooms.

Aided by oxygen, the mushrooms mature and release spores from their caps, repeating the life cycle.

As home growers, we begin with *substrate*, the growing medium, inside a sealed plastic bag. The substrate is a formula usually combining a grain such as corn kernels or rye berries with dried coconut husk, also known as *coco coir*.

The substrate has been sterilized and prepared with enough water to maintain sufficient moisture for healthy mycelial growth.

Grow bags come with a filter patch. These have tiny holes in them, typically 3 or 5 microns in size. This is just large enough to allow gases to slowly move in and out of the bag as temperature and pressure change in the environment. But the holes are not large enough to freely let fresh air in, which helps maintain a high carbon dioxide concentration.

Many online retailers today sell pre-made grow bags. They also sell syringes filled with either mushroom spores or mycelium for injecting into the bags. Syringes are specific to the strain of mushroom you desire.

There are many available strains of psilocybin mushrooms. The most recommended one for beginners is called Golden Teacher. But there are others, such as Amazonian, Ecuadorian, Cambodian, Penis Envy, Albino Penis Envy, Stargazer, Bluey Vuitton, Jedi Mind Fuck, etc. Cultivators have been very creative in developing unique strains and naming them too!

In the first stage of growing, you'll "inoculate" (inject) your grow bag using the syringe. Syringes with mycelium will produce growth faster than syringes with spores because they've already skipped the stage of waiting for spores to combine to produce mycelium.

After inoculation, you'll wait several weeks for mycelium to spread throughout the substrate. During this time, your bag only needs a relatively dark, room-temperature environment. For example, a bedroom closet.

When that stage is complete, you'll introduce the bag to *fruiting conditions.*

Mimicking nature's process, you'll open the bag to allow fresh air, especially oxygen, to enter the bag and signal the mycelium to begin growing mushrooms.

From this point on, you'll open the bag twice a day to reintroduce fresh air. You'll periodically spray the sides of the bag with water. Ideally, you'll use distilled water to reduce the chance of mold infestation.

The bag should be moved to a space in your home where it receives ambient light during the day. Artificial light is fine. Avoid direct sunlight. Darkness at night is fine. The bag should always be at room temperature, not too cold or hot.

Pins, baby mushrooms, should appear within a couple of weeks, maturing a week or two from that point. When the mushrooms are mature, you will harvest them, dry them, and keep them in airtight containers for long-term storage.

The following sections include materials lists, a general timeline, and specific, step-by-step instructions with photos for using your grow bag.

Some retailers are better than others for various reasons. I have had great results ordering from my local vendors. Some have storefronts which I recommend visiting because then you can ask them for personal guidance about growing and about the various strains they carry.

Since spores don't contain psilocybin, they're generally legal to sell and ship via the postal service.

Just think, you could grow all the mushrooms you'll ever need within two or three months, in the safety and privacy of your own home.

MATERIALS AND EQUIPMENT

- One pre-made, sterilized *grow bag* available from many online sellers. Bags are typically between 3 and 5 lbs. Various grains can be used in the bottom layer, such as corn kernels, rye berries, or millet. Be sure the grow bag you order is specifically formulated for psilocybin mushrooms since culinary mushrooms use different substrates such as wood or straw.

- One syringe filled with either spores or mycelium of the strain of your choice. Syringes usually come in 10 or 12 cc (cubic centimeters) sizes with a sterilized needle.

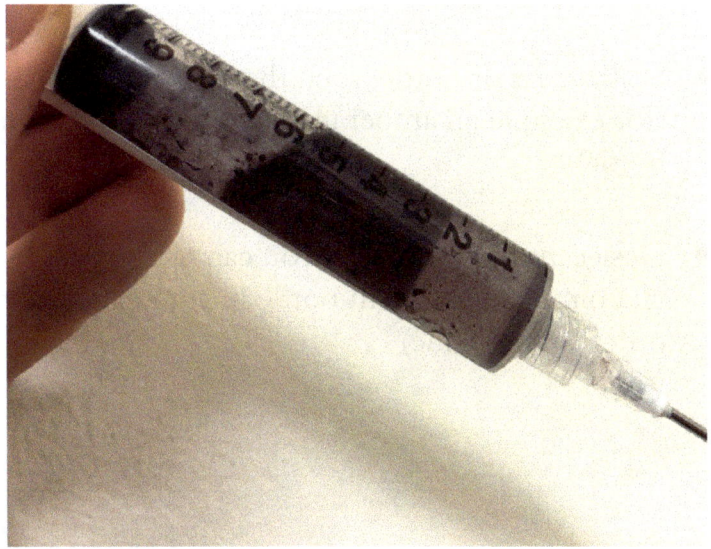

- 70% Isopropyl alcohol

- Cotton swabs for applying the alcohol (or you can purchase alcohol in a spray bottle).

- One spray bottle filled with distilled water (distilled water reduces the chance of mold infestation).

- Still air box (optional, described later)

- Face mask

- Duct tape, Scotch tape, or packing tape

EQUIPMENT FOR HARVESTING AND STORAGE

- Vegetable dehydrator

- Coffee grinder

- Sealable jar or bottle, such that can block UV light (for example an amber glass jar or opaque vitamin bottle)

- Desiccant packet (which you can take from a vitamin or supplement bottle in your cabinet or order some online)

GENERAL TIMELINE FROM START TO HARVEST

Details of each stage will be described in the next section.

A. Day 1: Inoculate (inject) your grow bag with the spores or mycelium from the syringe.

B. One to two weeks after A: "shake and break."

C. Two to three weeks after B: Colonization, when mycelium spreads throughout the substrate.

D. After C is complete: Introduction of fruiting conditions, with daily fanning and misting as necessary.

E. Two to four weeks after D: Pins appear, developing into mature mushrooms, at which point they are harvested, dried, and stored for future use.

F. Optional: Second "flush" to double the yield from your grow bag.

Total time: Eight to ten weeks.

DETAILED INSTRUCTIONS FOR GROWING

Step 1: After receiving your syringe and grow bag.

If you receive your syringe and grow bag sooner than when you're able to use them, store the syringe either at room temperature if you'll use it within a few days or in the refrigerator if longer, but **don't** freeze it.

Store your grow bag in a clean environment at room temperature.

Step 2: Inoculating the grow bag.

This step should be performed in a <u>clean</u> room. Avoid rooms where mold has been identified in the walls or under sinks. Turn off your air conditioning or heating system and close the windows to stop the flow of air. Let the air settle for a few minutes.

Optional: Using a still air box.

As an extra precaution against mold infestation, you can use a still air box. To make a still air box, take a large, <u>clear</u> plastic tub and cut two holes in one side, large enough for your hands and forearms to fit through. The tub will be upside down during use.

Place your grow bag, syringe, alcohol, and wipes inside the box. Spray any kind of mold-killing disinfectant inside

Path of the Golden Teacher

the box (through one of the arm holes) to clean the environment inside.

In the picture below, Sean wipes down the inside of the still air box with alcohol instead of using disinfectant spray. Either method is fine.

His gloved hands reaching inside the still air box, Sean injects jars instead of a grow bag using a spore syringe. The jar method is described in his book *Blue Thumb*.

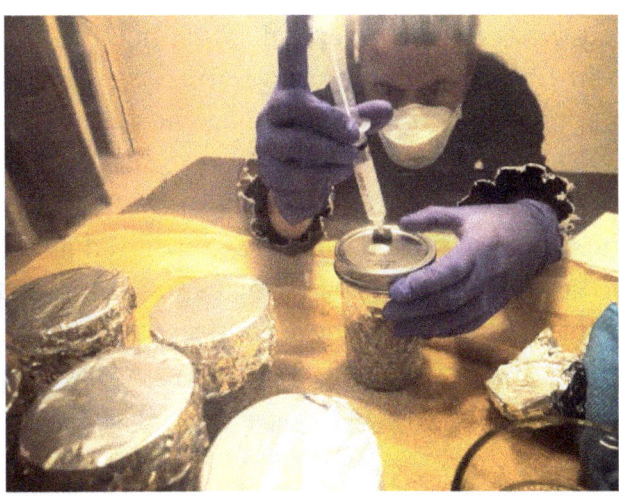

Detailed Instructions for Growing

The next steps are the same with or without a still air box.

Wear a mask to cover your nose and mouth to prevent oral pathogens from contacting the syringe or injection point on the bag.

Begin by washing your hands and wiping them clean with isopropyl alcohol (or use gloves and wipe them with alcohol).

Wipe the front surface of the bag with alcohol, especially the bottom half where you'll insert the needle.

Before you attach the needle to the end of the syringe, wipe down the syringe's plastic body and plunger with alcohol.

Open the needle's wrapper, only exposing the end where the attachment for the syringe is located. Then remove the small end cap from the syringe, attaching the needle.

Now that the syringe is attached to the needle, draw the needle out from its wrapper and immediately insert it into the bag at the layer of grain (popcorn kernels, for example).

In the next photo, note the needle is inserted at the grain layer of the bag. This bag had a black injection port attached to it, indicating where to insert the needle. Your bag may not have an injection port, as it is not necessary.

While emptying the entire syringe into the grain layer, move the needle to spread the fluid to either side as well as the center. Allow some of the fluid to be squirted just beneath the plastic. This will allow new mycelial growth to be visible.

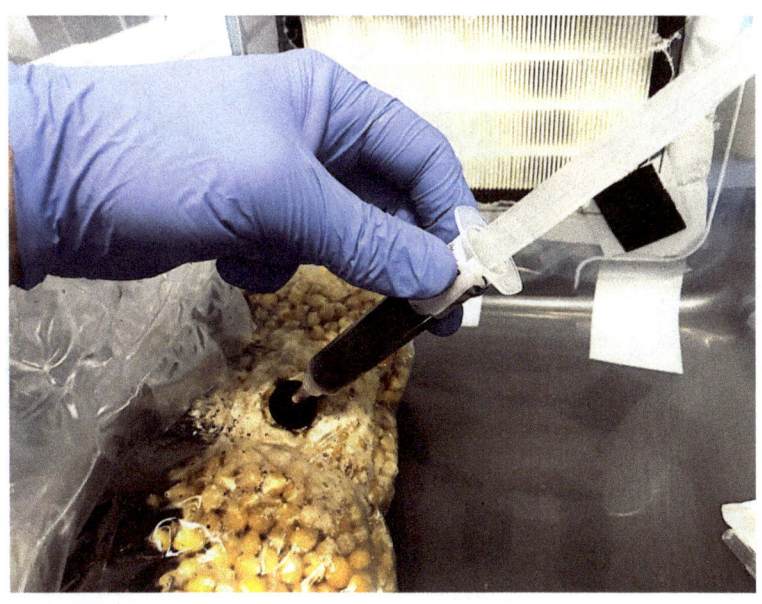

After emptying the syringe inside the bag, seal the hole with Scotch tape, duct tape, or packing tape.

Place the bag someplace dark at normal room temperature, somewhere between 68 and 75 degrees. Colder than that, and the mycelium may not grow, or it will grow slowly. Warmer than that could be advantageous for mold.

After ten to fourteen days, you many notice a large patch of white mycelium growing at the grain layer. It should cover at least 20% of the visible grain layer before doing "shake and break."

Detailed Instructions for Growing

Step 3: Shake and break.

This photo shows a grow bag ready for *shake and break*. The encircled area shows the wispy white threads of mycelium spreading across the grain.

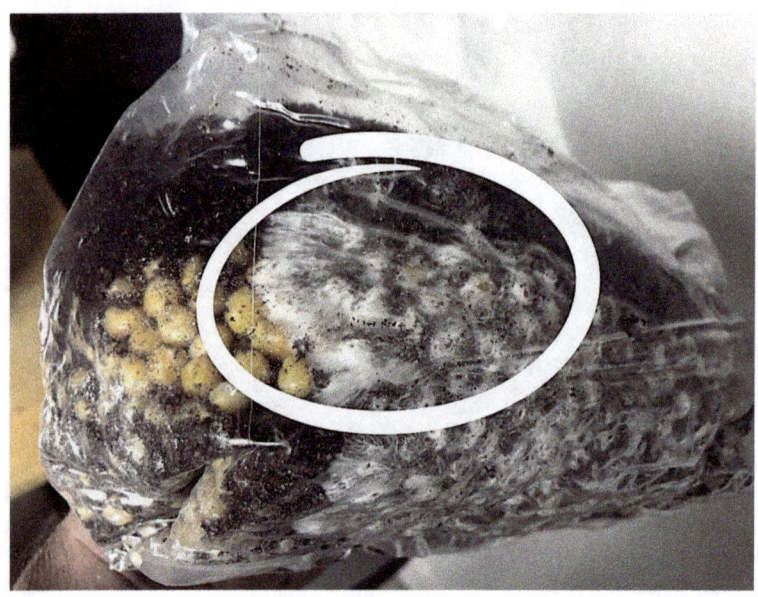

Gently massage the bag to break apart the grain layer and mycelium, mixing the grain into the darker substrate on top. You can also shake the bag and turn it upside down to thoroughly mix its contents.

Return the bag to where it was stored before and wait until the mycelium has spread throughout the mixed substrate.

The mycelium will seem to have disappeared after mixing the bag, but don't worry. You've dispersed it so that it will spread throughout the whole bag much faster than if you hadn't done shake and break. You should see new mycelial growth within a week.

Step 4: Waiting for full colonization.

It can take two, three, or even four weeks for the mycelium to entirely cover the substrate. It will be time to introduce fruiting conditions when either one of the following occurs:

- The mycelium has thoroughly covered the sides, top, bottom, front, and back of the substate in the bag. Small patches of dark substrate are fine.

- Pins (very young mushrooms) have started growing from the mycelium. These usually first appear on the sides of the bag instead of on top.

Step 5: Introducing fruiting conditions.

To introduce fruiting conditions, cut open the top of the bag after wiping it down with alcohol. The scissors should also be cleansed with alcohol.

Spread the sides apart and unfold the gussets (folds) to expand it and draw in fresh oxygen. Then fold the top over and use clips to close it (next photo).

Detailed Instructions for Growing

Then, snip a small hole on the high on one side of the bag, and another small hole low on the opposite side, just **above** the substrate layer. This will allow a passive flow of fresh air through the bag.

<-- Snipping a small hole, upper left side of bag.

--> Snipping a small hole, lower right side of bag.

Keep the bag somewhere it will be exposed to gentle lighting during the day (darkness at night is fine) at normal room temperature. Avoid direct sunlight. Artificial light is sufficient.

Step 6: Daily fresh air and misting as needed.

Twice a day, open the top of the bag and pull the sides apart a few times to draw in fresh air, particularly oxygen. This should only take a couple of seconds.

If you notice that the sides of the bag are dry, spray distilled water onto the plastic. <u>Don't overspray</u>. <u>Don't spray the mycelium directly.</u> If water begins to pool along the edges of the bag, this will be advantageous to mold growth. You just want to see droplets of water clinging to the sides of the bag.

Grow bags are good at maintaining humidity, so it's possible you won't need to spray very often at all.

Pins (baby mushrooms) are likely to appear on the sides of the bag within one to two weeks if they haven't already appeared by now.

Step 7: Managing stalled growth.

If you introduced fruiting conditions before pins appeared, and if two weeks later pins <u>still have not appeared,</u> you can try the following before giving up:

Place the bag in a bowl and fill the bag with enough distilled water to submerge the substrate. Since you've

Detailed Instructions for Growing

snipped a small hole on one side of the bag just above the substrate, the water will leak out at that level. This is why you've placed the bag in a bowl.

Place the bowl inside your refrigerator. The bag should be folded at the top and kept closed with clips.

Leave the bowl in the refrigerator for six hours.

After six hours, pour the water out of the bag, and put it back into fruiting conditions, fanning it twice a day, and misting the sides with purified water only when the sides appear dry.

Pins should appear within two weeks and take one to two more weeks to mature.

This picture shows mushrooms almost fully mature inside a grow bag. The larger ones are ready for harvesting. The amount shown will yield enough for multiple psilocybin journeys.

Step 8: Harvesting your mushrooms.

You might notice some of the mushrooms in the bag mature much faster than others. It's perfectly alright to harvest the large ones while leaving the others to continue growing.

The best time to harvest a mushroom is before the cap fully opens. If you wait too long, it will release its spores, which can be a bit messy. Waiting until the cap fully opens does not change the level of psilocybin in the mushroom, so there's no advantage to it.

To harvest a mushroom, simply reach into the bag and gently grasp the mushroom by its *stipe* (the stem) pulling and twisting it away from the mycelium. Make sure your hand is very clean when reaching into the bag so as not to introduce mold spores from your skin.

Psilocybin mushrooms bruise with a dark blue tint within a minute of being handled. This is normal. After harvesting, you can place them on a white surface and watch the change occur moment-by-moment.

If you harvest mature mushrooms while leaving younger ones in the bag to continue growing, dry the harvested ones immediately and place them in storage (an airtight jar or bottle).

Detailed Instructions for Growing

Step 9: Drying your mushrooms.

Before drying your mushrooms, scrape the ends of their stipes clean. Using a clean fingernail is sufficient.

Mushrooms shown growing, after being cleaned, and in the vegetable dehydrator. Photos from *Blue Thumb: How to Grow Psilocybin Mushrooms at Home (second edition).*

Mushrooms are 90% water, so they shrink considerably when dried.

Mushrooms should be **cracker dry** before being placed in storage. This means they should snap like a cracker. If they bend at all, that means there is still moisture inside. Storing them this way could lead to rot or mold.

Set your dehydrator to 130-140 degrees and let it run for at least 12 hours, or overnight. If the mushrooms aren't cracker dry afterward, give them several more hours in the dehydrator until they are.

Step 10: Storing your mushrooms.

Long-term air exposure can degrade psilocybin. Therefore, its best to keep the dried mushrooms intact inside a jar/bottle until you're ready to consume them, instead of grinding them into powder right away. Wait until you're ready to consume them before using a coffee grinder to pulverize them.

It's alright to pulverize enough for several weeks or months of a microdosing regimen for convenient daily use. The potency won't degrade very much during that period.

Whether you store you mushrooms whole or as powder, place a desiccant packet in the jar/bottle to help keep them dry. Mushroom powder easily absorbs humidity, so don't leave the container open for very long when using it, especially if you live in a humid environment.

Store your container at room temperature. If you use a clear glass bottle, keep it away from UV light, which can degrade psilocybin over time.

Detailed Instructions for Growing

The following picture shows mushrooms stored in an amber jar (to block UV light) after being ground into powder with an ordinary coffee grinder. Note the desiccant packets inside to maintain dryness. Amber jars and food-safe desiccant packets can be ordered online.

Step 11: Double your yield with a second flush.

It's possible to grow a second flush of mushrooms from the substrate after your first harvest. To do that, follow the same process described earlier, in Step 7, Managing Stalled Growth.

Place the bag in a bowl and fill the bag with enough distilled water to submerge the substrate. Since you've snipped a small hole on one side of the bag just above the substrate, the water will leak out at that level. This is why you've placed the bag in a bowl.

Place the bowl inside your refrigerator. The bag should be folded at the top and kept closed with clips.

Leave the bowl in the refrigerator for six hours.

After six hours, pour the water out of the bag, and put it back into fruiting conditions, fanning it twice a day, and misting the sides with purified water only when the sides appear dry.

Your second flush of mushrooms should begin to grow within two weeks and take one to two more weeks to mature.

A third flush is unlikely using a grow bag. But four or even five flushes are possible with a monotub, as described in *Blue Thumb*.

DEALING WITH MOLD

Mold is an unfortunate yet expected aspect of growing mushrooms. Every grower understands it's inevitable that from time to time, mold will spoil a bag or monotub. Mold can appear at the earliest stage, soon after inoculating your bag. Or it could appear later when mycelium has begun to grow. It could even appear afterward when mushrooms have begun to mature, though it's less likely at this stage since mycelium has an immune system of sorts.

Mold can appear blue, green, pink, or red. A grayish-white type of mold called "cobweb mold" can also appear on the surface.

Blue or aquamarine on your substrate doesn't always indicate mold. When mycelium is bruised, typically from handling, it turns blue, the same way its mushrooms do. I recently noticed a small patch of blue in one of my grow bags but noticed it was directly beneath a crease in the bag. I waited a couple of days to see if it spread (as mold would), but it didn't. I realized that every time I lifted the bag, the tension on the bag pulled the crease against the mycelium, bruising that one spot.

Thankfully, I waited long enough to determine it was only a bruise and not mold, preventing me from unnecessarily throwing it out.

If you're ever unsure if it's mold, take the bag outside and open it. Your nose will tell you for sure, as mold smells foul, funky, or sickly. Healthy mycelium smells earthy, nutty, mushroomy, and clean.

Never open a suspicious bag indoors. You will inadvertently release mold spores into your environment. If you have multiple bags or monotubs growing, the mold spores could put them at risk.

Because of the risk of mold, many growers prefer to grow two or three bags or monotubs at a time. Therefore, if one goes bad, hopefully the other kits will remain uncontaminated and succeed.

When you're finished with the substrate it can simply be buried in your garden or composted. If you live in a warm, humid area, you might discover new mushrooms coming up in your garden a couple of weeks later.

There is one countermeasure if you catch mold in the earliest stages once your bag or monotub is open. Spray it with 3% hydrogen peroxide. Spray the area once a day for two or three days until it's gone. The hydrogen peroxide won't harm the mycelium. But if the mold continues to grow, it's best to dispose of the entire substrate and start over.

If mushrooms have already started to grow and there is evidence of mold on them or even if you only suspect they could be harboring mold, do not consume them. It's not worth the risk of becoming seriously ill.

INTRODUCTION TO MICRODOSING

The term *microdosing* is used differently depending on who you ask or where you read it.

For one person, microdosing means taking a small dose, but large enough to feel a substantial shift in perception with heightened emotionality. Someone may take this amount for recreation, such as being at a party or concert. But in our context, this is *not* microdosing.

Here, we'll define microdosing as taking a *sub-perceptual* dose on a pre-determined schedule for a period lasting several months.

Sub-perceptual means an amount that does not affect your perception in any way. You should be as clear-headed as usual after consuming your sub-perceptual dose. This way, you can still drive a car, go to work, and manage any tasks you're responsible for in a sober fashion.

There are certain changes one would eventually feel, however. Ideally, taking psilocybin in small quantities over a long period will stimulate neuronal growth in the brain, producing the following desired effects:

- decreased anxiety and depression
- increased base level of happiness or contentment
- increased ability to let go when irritating events occur
- increased creativity and intuition
- increased sensitivity to and openness toward one's emotions

Microdosing may start to show benefits after staying on schedule for 4-6 weeks. These effects are based on real changes occurring in the brain, which take time to occur.

Remember, if you're using psilocybin to *instantly* feel different or change your perceptions, that is *not* microdosing. I've heard of novices taking an "extra" dose right before public speaking engagements, job interviews, and group activities, all in the hopes of improving their performance and effectiveness. The results were not good, to say the least.

Microdosing is a practice of patience and consistency. And since it's a time for stimulating neuronal growth, we can help the process by choosing supportive daily activities.

It's a great time to practice daily meditation (or something similar), spend more time in nature, watch less television, reduce social media, and avoid unhealthy depressants like alcohol. Microdosing isn't a silver bullet, so we must combine it with self-improvement activities.

Microdosing is also an opportunity to determine if your body can receive psilocybin without ill effects before taking a journey dose.

Some people develop headaches, hives/rash, or stomach issues after taking a microdose. Therefore, not only is microdosing contraindicated for them, but taking a journey dose is as well. If it doesn't feel good in small amounts, it'll feel terrible in large ones.

Introduction to Microdosing

It's not worth the risk of enduring multiple bouts of vomiting and a pounding headache for several hours while hallucinating.

And after increasing their emotional sensitivity, some microdosers realize they prefer *not* to feel their emotions quite so strongly and choose to stop.

The point is psilocybin isn't for everyone. But microdosing is a relatively safe way to find out if it's for you.

Specifics on how to determine your ideal dose, choosing a schedule, and how to take it are given later in this section.

You might experiment with taking it in the morning one day, and the next at bedtime. Since it stimulates neuronal growth, and since we do a lot of that growth in deep sleep, taking it at bedtime may better help the brain develop new pathways to deal with daytime events and stress, aiding in learning.

Taking it in the evening can also make your dreams more vivid and memorable. But if it disturbs your sleep, stick to taking it in the morning instead.

Above all, for this to be effective, you've got to stay on schedule. Just taking it randomly "once in a while" won't do much.

You'll find a sample journal entry later in this section. Taking a scientific approach toward your microdosing experience can be beneficial. You can do this by recording how you feel every day. Over time, you'll review your journal entries and determine if there has been a significant change in your day-to-day experience.

I experienced two unexpected specific side effects which you should be aware of. Neither occurred immediately, but only after several two-to-three-month cycles of microdosing.

The first one involved my occasional use of alcohol. I've never been a heavy drinker. When I did drink, it was typically with my wife as a prelude to dinner on a rare evening when we were home at the same time. We always split a single bottle of wine, two glasses each, usually white, but sometimes red.

At this point in my life, we enjoyed this ritual between two and four times a month, which meant I was only drinking between four and eight glasses of wine in a thirty days.

However, now that I was microdosing, my body's relationship to alcohol changed. Subtle flavors aside, the flavor of ethanol was pronounced, and I found it distasteful. My body would slightly recoil as I took each sip. Even though "I" wanted to drink it, my body did not.

As if to make its point clearer, my body began communicating more severely. It became a certainty that on a day immediately following the consumption of a glass or two of wine, I would have diarrhea.

This reminded me of when, in my thirties, I was in the process of quitting smoking nicotine, which is one of the hardest things I've ever done. Of significant help was seeing an acupuncturist. She installed several needles in my ear and elsewhere. Then, I lay on the treatment table for nearly an hour letting the needles do their thing.

The next time I inhaled a cigarette, I almost gagged.

The flavor was disgusting. I'd never had such a taste of foulness in my mouth before. At first, I thought it was just that particular cigarette. So, I tried another, and it was just as bad. Somehow, acupuncture altered how my mind, nose, and tongue experienced tobacco.

Now, with alcohol, the message finally made it through my thick skull, and I decided not to drink anymore. These days, silly me occasionally thinks, "Oh, it'll be okay since it's been so long since my last glass of wine," only to be reminded of my body's message the next day while sitting on the toilet.

Alcohol isn't just bad for people who are addicted to it. It's bad for everybody, even "only occasional" drinkers. I could no longer pretend this fact didn't apply to me as much as everyone else.

Introduction to Microdosing

The second side effect of microdosing came as a subtle cue from my body to stop drinking caffeine. I've been drinking caffeinated coffee since childhood and had never thought there was a reason to stop. Naturally, I was addicted to it, evidenced by slight headaches and sluggishness whenever I was unable to have my usual mid-afternoon cup of java.

Over a couple of weeks, I gradually noticed that I was unintentionally leaving my first cup of morning coffee unfinished. I was also forgoing my usual second cup for the morning. This was not a conscious choice. Instead, it was as if I had simply forgotten to pour it. The desire was gone. I was also leaving my afternoon cup unfinished.

I continued having my first morning cup, but stopped pouring the second one, knowing it would only go to waste. I also stopped making the afternoon one. It was around this time when it finally dawned on me, "I think my body is done with caffeine."

After that realization, I switched to decaffeinated coffee. I still love the flavor, and I enjoy the ritual of drinking the delicious beverage to mark a day's transition periods.

The curious thing is that I didn't get any headaches when I stopped. My body had no more use for the stimulant, and I believe microdosing psilocybin was an important part of that change.

Because of these two unintended yet beneficial side effects, I have no doubt about recent reports that psilocybin can help people recover from addiction to alcohol and other substances.

Some people take Lion's mane mushroom supplements while microdosing psilocybin because reports indicate Lion's mane also has positive effects on cognitive functioning. Taking the mushrooms together for a common purpose is called *stacking*.

In the year before I began microdosing, I noticed that it was getting harder for me to remember where I'd parked my car when grocery shopping. It was happening so often that I was becoming concerned about my memory.

But after several months of stacking psilocybin with Lion's mane, I stopped forgetting. I could exit the grocery store and instantly recall where I'd parked.

I don't know whether the credit should go to the psilocybin or the Lion's mane, or to stacking them. It could also be the placebo effect given that I consciously anticipated their potential effects. Still, I'm grateful for those effects no matter the true cause.

Lion's mane is legal everywhere and supplements are sold in many groceries and health food stores, typically in capsules. It's also sold fresh and whole in the produce section. Restaurants use it as a vegetarian substitute for crab and lobster.

The following chapters will guide you in determining your ideal dosage for microdosing, how to consume it, on what schedule, and more.

The recommended videos below are specific to microdosing:

Science and Nonduality (Apr. 18, 2019). *The Remarkable Results of Microdosing with James Fadiman* – on YouTube

Science and Nonduality (Apr. 2, 2018). *Microdosing a Really Good Day: Ayelet Waldman* – on YouTube

HOW TO DETERMINE YOUR IDEAL MICRODOSE

You might start with 0.05 grams (1/20th of a gram) as your dose on the first day. If you feel anything unusual within an hour, that means the next day you should take it down to 0.04 or 0.03 and see if you still feel anything. Don't drive a car or attend any important meetings if you feel a perceptual shift.

But if you feel absolutely nothing after taking the 0.05 grams, the following day take it up to 0.06 or 0.07 grams and see how that goes.

Day by day, week by week, take it up a little more. But be sure not to take any on the off days of your chosen microdosing schedule (see the chapter *Your Microdosing Schedule*).

When you feel a "slightly off" feeling, or slightly altered perception, slightly anxious, or suspect you should *not* drive a vehicle, that means it's no longer a microdose. At that point, revert to the previous day's dose that didn't cause any significant changes in perception or "slightly off" feelings.

That lower, sub-perceptual dose is your ideal microdose for as long as you use the same supply.

Some people get up to around 0.10 grams before feeling like they crossed the line. But please don't use that number as any type of goal or standard to be met. Your only goal should be to find the dose that is appropriate to you.

But the term "sub-perceptual" is misleading by indicating you shouldn't perceive anything at all. The fact is you will notice some differences. Daily irritations like bad drivers on the highway or whether someone left the toilet seat up (or down) may not bug you as much, if at all.

You might feel more creative at work or with a hobby. And you'll be more sensitive to your emotions. If you have a favorite song that stirs your heart, you might feel that song a little more deeply.

You might also notice a pleasant sensation either in one part of your body or throughout. I experience the sensation as "comfortable" or "a little bit soft and squishy." I believe it reflects a physical release of tension.

Still, there *is* a difference between those changes and crossing the line into **macro** dosing. Personal experience is the best way to determine that difference.

Every time you grow new mushrooms, you can use a test kit before consuming them to know how potent the powder is.[30] If it's a lot weaker, then you'll know to increase your starting dose by a few milligrams. If it's a lot stronger, then start with less.

I recently found a website in which the blogger explicitly recommended 0.35 grams for microdosing. They reasoned that since an "average" hallucinogenic dose is 3.5 grams, 1/10th of that (0.35 grams) would be appropriate for microdosing. The calculation of 1/10th to 1/20th of a hallucinogenic dose to determine a microdose is widely referenced in books and the internet.

---

[30] See the following chapter, *How to Test for Potency*.

Yet, the blogger didn't give any consideration for potency. For example, with a batch I recently tested with an at-home test kit, taking 0.35 grams would be foolish and could leave the microdoser feeling very uncomfortable the rest of the day, easily crossing the line into macro dosing.

The blogger also didn't consider an individual's unique sensitivity to psilocybin. Using me as an example, 0.1 grams from a recent grow was my upper limit since my priority as a microdoser was to keep it sub-perceptual.

It's wrong to assume that a person weighing 250 lbs. will experience 0.08 grams differently than a person weighing 140 lbs. Both of their brains weigh similarly, around 3 lbs. And no matter how long it takes to circulate through the body, especially the liver, the brain is the final destination.

When it comes to psilocybin mushrooms, there is no such thing as an "average" dose. Every batch of powdered mushrooms has a different potency. And every person has their unique sensitivity to it.

I believe this was a case of a blogger reusing advice they found elsewhere on the internet, without having personally experienced what they wrote about.

Please be careful when taking advice from bloggers who you don't personally know and trust. Many people blog for income by writing about topics they can intersperse with affiliate links. When you click on a shopping link on their site for a vegetable dehydrator, a sterilized grain bag, vermiculite, capsule fillers, etc., they earn a small royalty as an affiliate for whoever the retailer is.

Professional bloggers write about hot topics so they can get more clicks. So, although they can't be experts at everything, that doesn't stop them from writing about…well, just about everything.

That type of blogging poses a risk to unsuspecting and uneducated readers. It also does nothing to support our efforts to make political, legal, and social inroads for public access to psilocybin by modeling responsible use.

Society and its lawmakers trust us to responsibly dose our daily servings of alcohol, nicotine, caffeine, sugar, marijuana, pain pills, online gambling, food supplements, and social media.

Let's show them we're perfectly capable of measuring our psilocybin doses for wellness and spiritual development without a doctor's prescription, or anybody else's permission.

HOW TO TEST FOR POTENCY

Measuring your dosage before consumption is part of *harm reduction*.

That phrase encompasses supporting your health goals, maintaining personal responsibility and safety, and encouraging lawmakers, politicians, and society at large to continue reviewing the scientific data regarding its medical effectiveness for mental health.

Responsible and effective use includes knowing how potent your psilocybin is. Imagine you're about to finish your current supply of dried mushrooms, and you recently harvested a new grow bag. Your new crop finished drying and you powdered it and stored it away.

It would be wrong to automatically start using the same dose with the new batch as the old one. 0.08 grams may have kept things "sub-perceptual" before.

But with the new batch, which may be significantly more potent, 0.08 grams crosses the line, making you feel "off" or slightly anxious instead of feeling steady and positive. This is no longer microdosing.

Path of the Golden Teacher

Therefore, testing a tiny portion of your powdered supply before consuming it is the smart thing to do. As of this writing, a German company named Miraculix[31] has made an affordable home-test kit available. If you live in the United States, scroll down on their site and click on the "Shipping and Delivery" link to find their U.S. distributor.

I recommend testing each new batch of dried psilocybin powder before starting a new microdosing regimen or before taking a journey dose.

Testing the potency will help you decide whether to alter your dose when using a new supply of mushroom powder and by how much.

The picture below shows the home test kit's contents.[32]

---

[31] www.miraculix-lab.de/en. As of the time of this publication, U.S. orders can be placed through www.QTests.org

[32] Find a video of me showing how to use the test kit at https://vimeo.com/858881411 or going to Vimeo.com and searching for *Blue Thumb Psilocybin Club*.

How to Test for Potency

The test result below is given by comparing the testing solution to a graphic scale. Notice that the solution's dark tone indicates the highest potency.

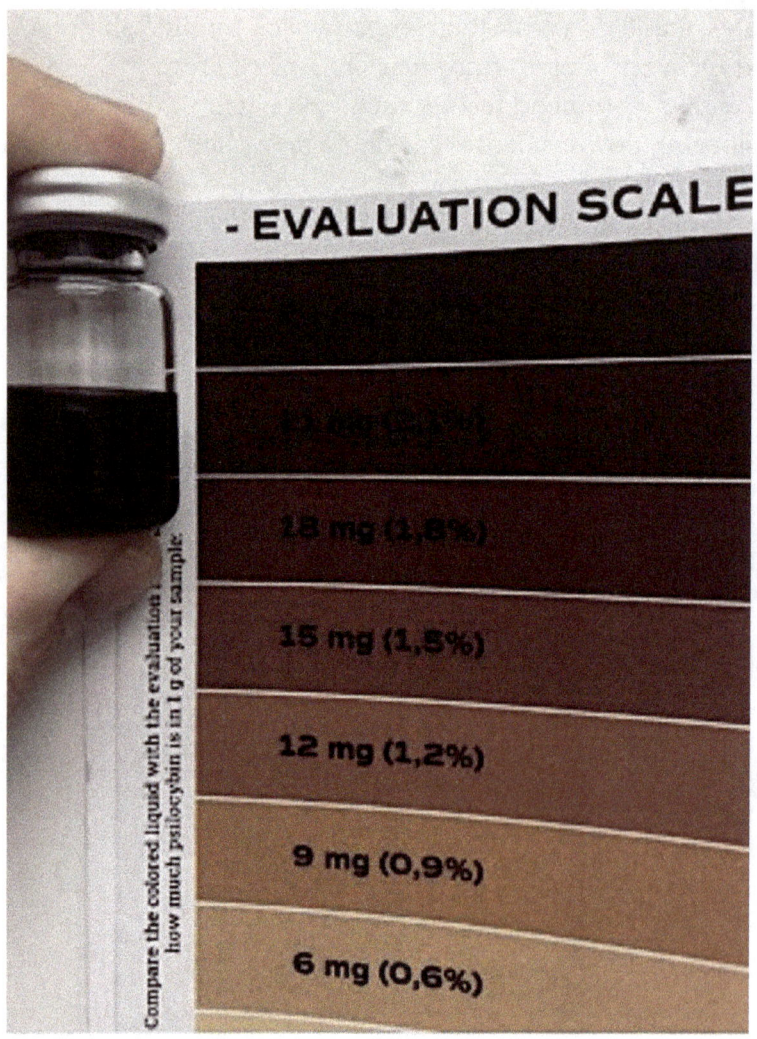

To learn how I made my batch so potent, see the chapter *The Secret to High Potency* in my book *Blue Thumb*.

USING A DIGITAL SCALE FOR MEASURING DOSAGE

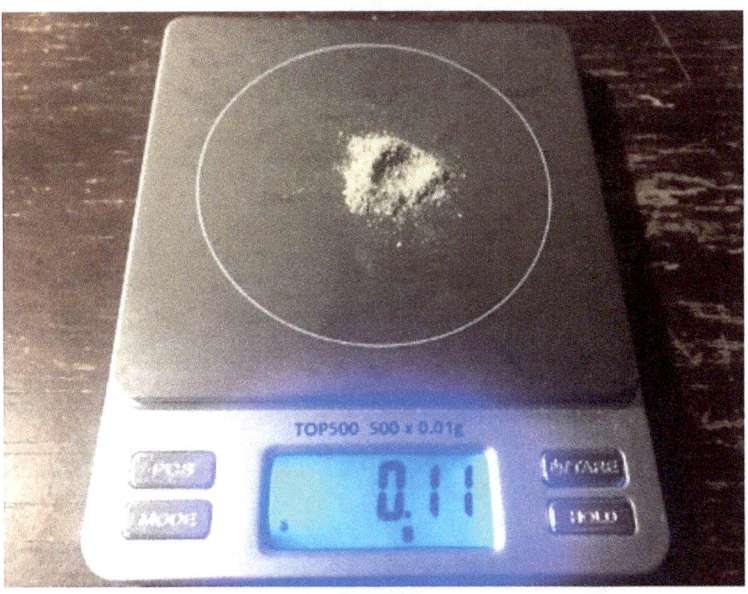

In microdosing, it's important to determine your optimal dose using a digital scale. There can be a significant experiential difference between 0.07 grams and 0.1 grams of dried psilocybin, depending on the potency of the powder and the unique sensitivity of the person. In microdosing, **accuracy matters**.

After you find your ideal dose, using a scale <u>every single time</u> helps you maintain accuracy.

A scale that only reads down to 0.1 grams, only tenths of a gram, isn't helpful for microdosing. You want a scale that reads to the 0.01-gram level, the hundredths of a gram, as in the picture above. Sidenote: if you plan on using DMT, you'll need a scale sensitive to 0.001 grams, or milligrams (see Part Four).

Again, there can be a significant difference between 0.1 grams and 0.07 grams, and not all scales can accurately measure that difference.

HOW TO CONSUME YOUR MICRODOSE

There are three different ways you can consume your home-grown, dried mushrooms. All assume you've used a coffee grinder to pulverize them.

The first is to fill empty capsules individually, by hand. Kits including special tools for doing this are available online. Search for "capsule filling tool kit." These kits are just sets of variously sized long, flat spoons and compactors to press the powder into capsules one at a time.

I used this method briefly, then stopped because it just took too much time and hassle to weigh the powder and fill capsules one at a time to make sure the dosage was the same in each one.

The second method is to use a multiple-capsule filling machine, also available online. Search for "capsule filler," "capsule filling tray," or "capsule filling machine." Although this allows you to fill multiple capsules at the same time, I don't trust that the same amount of powder will go into each capsule.

Since microdosing psilocybin **requires precision** when done responsibly, I don't like filling machines.

My favorite method is to simply scoop a tiny portion of powder onto my digital scale to determine the appropriate amount. Then, I dump the powder from the scale directly into my oatmeal, coffee, or hot chocolate. **There's no need for capsules at all.**

You can also add it to a smoothie, a cup of yogurt, or any other food that can be stirred to disguise the flavor since it's a little bit funky. The easiest method is to fill a glass with a small amount of water, dump the powder into it, and drink it down in a single gulp.

YOUR MICRODOSING SCHEDULE

Your body will develop tolerance to psilocybin after microdosing for several days. Therefore, the most important part of your schedule is to take days off from microdosing to prevent tolerance buildup.

Some suggest microdosing **four days in a row and then taking three days off**. Others suggest **one day on, two days off**. Still others recommend two days on, followed by two days off.

Whatever schedule you choose, write it down, and stick with it for at least two or three months. If you already make use of your phone or computer's calendar (and its automatic reminders and alerts), you should add your microdosing schedule to it to help you be consistent.

Recording your schedule will also help you be thoughtful and deliberate when considering altering your schedule and dose. When you make a change, stick with it long enough to determine whether it's working or if you should make another change.

Regardless of your schedule, you can learn a lot about yourself by keeping a daily microdosing journal. The example on the next two pages offers a framework for what you might record.

Notice near the top of the first page where it asks you to circle whether today is an "On-Day" or "Off-Day." This refers to whether you took a microdose today, or not. This would depend on the specific schedule you choose, for example, four days on & three off, or one day on & two off, etc.

DAILY MICRODOSING JOURNAL

Dedicate a blank notebook for recording the information below. Ideally, you'll do these reflections before bedtime, nightly.

Date:_____   Day of the Week:_____

Circle one:

Today is an On-Day   Today is an Off-Day

Time of day the dosage was taken:_____

Amount taken (for example, 0.08 grams):_____

How it was taken (tea, food, capsule, etc.):

General mood before taking the dose (if dosing today):

Mood changes after taking the dose throughout the remainder of the day:

Any positive, healing, productive or pleasant feelings, sensations, thoughts, or reactions/responses today?

Any strange, uncomfortable, unwanted, or out of the ordinary feelings, sensations, thoughts, or reactions/responses today?

Does it seem like you need to adjust your dose up or down next time?

If so, what should the next dosage measurement be?

* Small changes are recommended, for example going from 0.08 grams to 0.09 grams instead jumping from 0.08 to 0.1. Spend several days or weeks slowly dialing in your ideal dose, remembering to keep it sub-perceptual. If you experience altered perception, or something *beyond* a general uplift in mood, creativity, and calm, that's no longer microdosing, so back it down to the previous day's dose.

HOW TO DETERMINE YOUR IDEAL JOURNEY DOSE

In the previous section about finding your ideal microdose, I mentioned why there is no such thing as an "average" dose. Remember there are two reasons for this, the potency of the mushrooms being consumed (whole or as powder) and a person's unique sensitivity to psilocybin.

Therefore, statements like, "A therapeutic dose is three grams, and a 'hero' dose is five or more grams," are misguided and incomplete. The term "hero dose" is problematic because it appeals to some people's desire for accolades, machismo, and self-aggrandizement, causing them to take an unnecessarily larger dose.

Terence McKenna coined the term hero dose and defined it as a dose large enough to drastically alter one's perception of self and reality. Over time, the hero dose was equated to five grams, which is arbitrary, unhelpful, and even dangerous.

I have experienced powerful journeys including full-blown hallucinations on just *half a gram* of dried psilocybin powder, so I know large doses are not always necessary. Also, the larger the dose, the greater the chance of experiencing a challenging journey (a "bad trip").

I knew to take only half a gram because I had used a home test kit to test the mushroom powder's potency ahead of time[33]. The powder tested at the highest level. And I seem to be more sensitive to psilocybin than average simply due to my genetics.

The point is that choosing to take a certain dose based on arbitrary numbers recommended by a blogger, online discussion forum, or a stranger at the party is not the way to go.

Fortunately, there are two safer approaches for deciding how much to take on your first (or next) psilocybin journey. They begin on the next page.

Experienced users may think I'm being too careful, a worrywart. But I don't believe it's possible to be too careful when it comes to sharing information about psychedelics with the public.

---

[33] See the chapter *How to Test for Potency*.

How to Determine Your Ideal Journey Dose

Method 1: Multiply your ideal microdose.

In this method, it's assumed that you have been microdosing long enough to have determined your ideal microdose.

It's generally accepted that a microdose is somewhere between 1/10th and 1/20th of a journey dose. So, if you know your ideal microdose, you can multiply that amount ten and twenty times to find a range for your journey dose.

Here are some dosing calculations for easy reference:

	Journey Dose Range	
Microdose	Low End (x10)	High End (x20)
0.05 grams	0.5 grams	1 gram
0.06 grams	0.6 grams	1.2 grams
0.07 grams	0.7 grams	1.4 grams
0.08 grams	0.8 grams	1.6 grams
0.09 grams	0.9 grams	1.8 grams
0.10 grams	**1 gram**	**2 grams**
0.12 grams	1.2 grams	2.4 grams
0.14 grams	1.4 grams	2.8 grams
0.16 grams	1.6 grams	3.2 grams
0.18 grams	1.8 grams	3.6 grams
0.2 grams	2 grams	4 grams

But is this chart very helpful? I don't think so, considering that I based my half-gram dose (the one that sent me on a full psychedelic journey) on the fact that my ideal microdose at the time was 0.1 grams.

Note that I used the same powder for my journey that I was using for microdosing, so the potency was consistent. You should do the same for this method to work properly.

According to the chart on the previous page, I might have decided to take between 1 and 2 grams, instead of 0.5 grams.

That would have been two to four times the amount that I actually needed. And yes, there can be a noticeable difference in a journey's intensity between one and two grams.

Therefore, if I recalculated the chart on the previous page based on a person being **more sensitive than average**, and the psilocybin supply being above-average in potency, it would result in the following. Notice that the low end is the microdose multiplied by five, and the high end is the microdose multiplied by ten.

	Journey Dose Range	
Microdose	Low End (x5)	High End (x10)
0.05 grams	0.25 grams	0.5 gram
0.06 grams	0.3 grams	0.6 grams
0.07 grams	0.35 grams	0.7 grams
0.08 grams	0.4 grams	0.8 grams
0.09 grams	0.45 grams	0.9 grams
0.10 grams	**0.5 gram**	**1 grams**
0.12 grams	0.6 grams	1.2 grams
0.14 grams	0.7 grams	1.4 grams
0.16 grams	0.8 grams	1.6 grams
0.18 grams	0.9 grams	1.8 grams
0.2 grams	1 gram	2 grams

How to Determine Your Ideal Journey Dose

This chart makes more sense to me than the previous one. The best way for you to know if it makes sense for *you* is to spend several weeks determining your ideal microdose and then refer to these charts.

If you seem particularly sensitive to psilocybin, meaning your ideal microdose is somewhere under 0.07 grams (remember, microdosing means it's sub-perceptual), or you feel that you're generally sensitive to pharmaceutical medication, alcohol, caffeine, or other substances, you might want to use the second chart to calculate your journey dose and choose an amount closer to the low end.

An important attitude to keep is that it's better to be underwhelmed than overwhelmed during a journey because it is like a very long roller coaster ride. There's no getting off early. You're strapped in for the duration. So, start low, and go slow.

If afterward, you find yourself thinking, "I could have done more and had a better experience," that's great information to have.

Now you can base your next journey's dose on your personal experience rather than my or anybody else's charts, assuming the psilocybin you use next time is the same potency as the one you used before. You have the rest of your life to take more journeys, and they'll be even better because of your prior experience.

If you've run out of psilocybin, grow more, dry and powder it, and use a test kit to determine its potency (See the chapter *How to Test for Potency*). Then, find your ideal microdose with the new supply and refer to these charts again.

Method 2: If you don't know, start low.

You might not have microdosed before and are considering a psychedelic journey without having done so. A significant downside to that is that since you don't know how your body responds to a small dose you certainly won't know how it'll respond to a large one.

If it's possible for a tiny amount to give you a headache or cause an allergic response, imagine how much worse you might feel taking a journey dose. It could be quite uncomfortable, last several hours, and worst of all, it would come as a surprise.

For any number of reasons, you may choose not to microdose and prefer to go straight into journeying.

In that case, start low regardless of the powder's potency. I can't tell you what low means for you. For me, low means half a gram. As I said on the previous page, you might finish the journey feeling like it was too little, or like almost nothing happened. This is much better than having taken too much. The chapter *Boosting Your Journey* later here in Part Three will show you how to adjust your total intake while a journey is in progress.

The benefits to starting low are that it's safer and the next time you journey, you'll be able to choose a higher dosage based on prior experience.

HOW TO CONSUME YOUR JOURNEY DOSE

As you've probably seen in various documentaries of people going on journeys, there are different ways to consume the mushroom. Some people simply bite, chew, and swallow the dried mushrooms, chasing each bite with gulps of water. Some chop it up and mix it with honey, again chasing each bite with water just to get it down.

There's also "lemon tek," in which mushroom powder is placed in a shot glass. Lemon juice is added to it, and the whole mixture is taken in one shot. Because of the bitter flavor, it's not something to be sipped. The common thought is that the lemon's acidity makes the journey come up faster and more intensely while shortening its duration.

My favorite way to take the mushroom is to prepare a mixture of hot chocolate and ginger tea. I use ordinary hot chocolate from the grocery store, nothing fancy. The chocolate does a reasonable job of masking the funky mushroom flavor. The ginger tea helps with any nausea I might feel in the first hour or two after drinking it. Ginger also adds a spicy kick to the hot chocolate.

Simply pour the pre-weighed mushroom powder into your cup of hot ginger-chocolate tea and stir it with a spoon. It's normal for some of the powder to float to the surface after stirring.

Taking the mushroom this way makes it more enjoyable and easier to swallow. Also, you can take your time setting your intention and preparing yourself psychologically as you drink it.

BOOSTING YOUR JOURNEY

What if an hour passes after having taken your journey dose and the effects are quite weak? Are you stuck with that experience for the remainder of the journey? No.

You can boost your journey the following way. At the end of the first hour after consuming the mushroom (no longer than that), take an additional 30% to 50% of the initial dose. For example, if you took 1 gram initially, you could take another 0.3 to 0.5 grams to boost your experience.

If you don't experience a significant increase in your journey's intensity by the end of the second hour (one hour after taking a booster dose), do **not** take any more doses. Doing so will only extend the duration of your mediocre journey, but not increase its intensity.

There could be a neurological reason why you're not responding to the psilocybin, perhaps involving your serotonin receptors, past pharmaceutical use, or being burned out due to work, lifestyle, or unhealthy coping mechanisms.

There could also be a psychological reason for barely feeling anything. You might be blocking the psychedelic experience out of fear or an excessive, perhaps unconscious, need to maintain control.

This is unlikely to happen to those who complete all of the meditation series offered in the *Path*[34] before going on their journey, since meditation trains one to let go and be open to the most subtle experiences.

Still, I mention the possibility of blocking here because some of this book's readers may have no interest in doing the meditations. In their case, speaking to a therapist or counselor may be helpful before attempting a subsequent journey.

---

[34] Find it at www.WisdomWithin.space/PathOfTheGoldenTeacher

BETTER THAN AYAHUASCA AND PEYOTE

This chapter's title may raise a few eyebrows at first glance. But keep in mind this book is in part about harm reduction. Instead of reducing harm to oneself, this chapter discusses reducing harm to others.

North and south of the U.S.-Mexican border, indigenous cultures who have used peyote for traditional practices for many generations are now facing a dire shortage of the extremely slow-growing cactus.

In the 2020 paper *Peyote Crisis Confronting Modern Indigenous Peoples: The Declining Peyote Population and a Demand for Conservation*,[35] we learn that farming, mining, and modern infrastructure are destroying the fragile environment required for peyote to thrive.

And the other culprit is psychedelic tourism. Non-indigenous people hire guides to help them locate the cacti, and the tourists take as much as they can without considering the cultural needs of the indigenous people who still maintain an honorable relationship with the cactus. The 2022 docuseries, *How to Change Your Mind*[36] touches on this. Or you can read the book it's based on with the same title.

Non-indigenous people are also wreaking havoc in the Amazon through psychedelic tourism. The economic force of the dollar is driving the creation of healing centers through the collaboration (or coercion?) between entrepreneurs and shamans.

---

[35] Muneta, J. (December 23, 2020). *Peyote Crisis Confronting Modern Indigenous Peoples: The Declining Peyote Population and a Demand for Conservation.* American Indian Law Journal. Volume 9, Issue 1.

[36] Pollan, M., Gibney, A. (2022). *How to Change Your Mind.* Distributed by Netflix. https://michaelpollan.com/books/how-to-change-your-mind/

Some of the shamans are authentic and earnest. Others may have questionable credentials and even less honorable intentions.

Worse, authentic shamans are being forced out of their villages by aggressive, competitive market forces. To witness an example of this, watch the documentary *The Last Shaman*.[37] It should break your heart.

The point is that you can reduce the harm being done to entire cultures right now if you abstain from psychedelic tourism.

If a person believes they deserve to fly someplace exotic to experience healing at the cost of destroying ecosystems and indigenous people's access to their own medicine, I hope they will think twice.

Sometimes, healing begins with humility. And humility increases empathy. Then compassion.

There's no need to travel for plant medicine when you can easily grow psilocybin inside a bag or box in your living room without hurting vulnerable communities and our fragile planet.

---

[37] Degan, R. (2016). *The Last Shaman*. Distributed by Netflix. https://www.thelastshaman.com/

PART FOUR
CANNABIS & DMT

CANNABIS WITH MEDITATION AND PSILOCYBIN

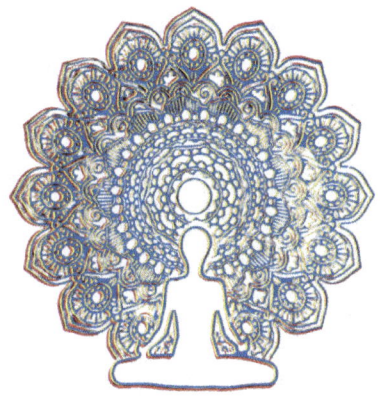

Cannabis has at least three potential roles to play in some people's exploration of psychedelics.

The first role we'll discuss is how it can assuage one's nausea after consuming psilocybin mushrooms and make the journey more enjoyable. Second, some people might benefit from using cannabis during the tail end of their psilocybin journey.

Finally, cannabis has hallucinogenic effects in some (not all) people, classifying it as a psychedelic. I'll share my personal experience of combining cannabis with meditation both when taken as a tincture and when vaped.

But first, we need to discuss contraindications, ways to take cannabis, and other things before talking about how to combine it with meditation and other psychedelics.

Cannabis with Meditation and Psilocybin

Contraindications for Cannabis

Because of cannabis' potential as a psychedelic, it's best to review the contraindications for psilocybin and apply them here. You can find them in Part Two.

Know that cannabis is difficult to categorize. Depending on dosage and on how your body responds to it, cannabis can also act as a depressant or a stimulant.[38] This explains why if you've ever been in a social situation where several people were using cannabis, one person may have become paranoid, anxious, or hyperactive while another became subdued, forgetful, or sleepy.

If you have a health condition or take a pharmaceutical medication that requires you to avoid stimulant or depressants, then you should probably avoid cannabis if it affects you in those ways.

And as always you should consult with your physician before using it.

How to Take Cannabis

Almost everyone knows that cannabis can be smoked in a joint, pipe, or bong. The benefit of smoking is the effect is so fast the user can moderate their intake by taking a hit and then waiting a while to see if they're getting the desired effect. If they're not, they just need to take another hit and wait a few more minutes. The downside to smoking is the negative effects on one's lungs from the harmful chemicals produced by burning the plant material.

Tinctures avoid using the lungs altogether. Tincture bottles come with graduated droppers so you can measure your dose before dropping the solution under your tongue

---

[38] Cherney, Kristeen. "Is Weed a Depressant, Stimulant, or Hallucinogen? Effects, Risks, More." *Healthline,* Healthline Media, 19 May 2023, www.healthline.com/health/is-weed-a-depressant.

and holding it there for several minutes. Various online resources say tinctures take effect within 15 to 30 minutes. But in my experience, the effect can take much longer to kick in.

Cannabis can also be eaten and is frequently sold in the form of gummies, chocolates, and even desserts. The downside is it can take a very long time, even hours, before the effects are felt, and they can be extremely strong. Edibles are frequently the cause of cannabis toxicity and can send frightened, inexperienced users to the hospital.

There is also the option of vaping "dry flower," which is different from using a liquid vape pen or cartridge. Pens and cartridges use liquid carriers such as vitamin E acetate or propylene glycol to dissolve THC. But there's no way to be sure what liquid is being used or its quality, and there are serious concerns about the long-term effect on one's lungs and overall health.

But *dry vaping* doesn't use a liquid carrier. And it doesn't burn the plant matter the way using a pipe, bong, or joint does. Instead, it heats the plant matter without combusting (burning) it. A dry vaporizer is like a small oven, heating the cannabis to vaporize the beneficial compounds without burning it and producing noxious smoke.

Of course, there is still some risk to the lungs with long-term use because a foreign substance is being inhaled, regardless of whether it's smoke or vapor.

As you'll read later in this chapter, vaping dry flower is some people's preferred method for using cannabis because the effects are immediate (under five minutes), it's smoke-free, and like smoking and tinctures, you can stop administering it once you get the desired effect.

The other benefit is when using an electric vaporizer there's no need to use a lighter. This is especially convenient

Cannabis with Meditation and Psilocybin

when using cannabis during meditation, especially if sitting in the dark or wearing a blindfold.[39]

Caution for first-time cannabis users

For a first-timer, combining two mind-altering substances will probably cause more problems and confusion than it will solve.

Remember that psychedelics amplify emotions and mental states. So, if someone uses cannabis right before a psilocybin journey and becomes paranoid or anxious, the risk is for those emotions to be greatly multiplied after the psilocybin takes effect. Imagine their heart rate increasing from the cannabis and its perception becoming "louder" or more intense during the psilocybin journey. How might someone react? These effects could easily lead to a challenging journey, a "bad trip."

In the last paragraph's example, the person's body responded to cannabis as if it were a stimulant. What if someone responds to cannabis as a depressant? In that case, the resultant confusion, dizziness, and lack of motor control could worsen once the psilocybin takes effect.

If you're considering using cannabis with psilocybin, you need to know whether it affects you as a depressant or a stimulant and consider the risks when those effects and your emotional responses to them are greatly intensified by the psychedelic.

It's best to become familiar with them separately before using them together.

Cannabis for psilocybin-related nausea

Cannabis is well-known for helping chemotherapy patients reduce nausea. Cannabis can also help reduce nausea

---

[39] Using a blindfold is highly recommended for those using the online meditation program.

when consuming psilocybin.[40] The results of a University of New Mexico study published in 2022 indicate that cannabis sativa and hybrid strains did better at reducing nausea than indica did. Also, THC outperformed CBD for nausea relief.

According to the study, relief can occur anywhere from five minutes to one hour after consuming THC. Therefore, using THC from five minutes to one hour before consuming psilocybin might be effective for reducing nausea afterward.

For predicting the speed of onset, vaping and smoking are recommended over edibles. You want to predict and control the intensity of the cannabis' effect especially when combining it with psilocybin, but you can't do that with edibles.

Experienced cannabis users will be able to gauge how much to take for nausea reduction without getting too high before consuming the psilocybin.

As I mentioned in the chapter *Preparation*, first-time psilocybin journeyers should opt for ginger, lemon tek, or good meal scheduling to reduce nausea instead of using cannabis, especially if they've never used it before.

Cannabis during the tail end of a psilocybin journey

As you'll see in the next section, cannabis's effect has some similarities to that of psilocybin, albeit far less pronounced. Because of these similarities, some people find them compatible and use cannabis to intensify their journey near its peak (around 2 hours after consuming psilocybin). Others use it toward the end (3-4 hours after consumption) to prolong the journey.[41]

---

[40] See http://news.unm.edu/news/cannabis-offers-mmediate-relief-from-symptoms-of-nausea-but-product-use-matters.

[41] https://www.healthline.com/health/substance-use/shrooms-and-weed#mixing-cannabis-and-mushrooms

Cannabis with Meditation and Psilocybin

I've never used cannabis to intensify or prolong a psilocybin journey because the experience always feels complete without it.

MEDITATING WITH CANNABIS

Note: Because the body develops tolerance to cannabis, the dosages mentioned in the following anecdotes should not be considered general recommendations. I am not a regular cannabis user, so I have no accumulated tolerance whenever I use it. Therefore, my dosages are smaller compared to what a regular user might need to get the same effect.

Part One: an anecdote with tincture

For this meditation session, I took one full dropper (1 ml) containing 35 mg of THC, 35 mg of CBD, and 35 mg of CBG. I figured if a standardized dose of THC is 10 mg, then this amount would certainly have pronounced physical and mental effects during my meditation.

Since a tincture takes longer than vaping or smoking to take effect, I started my session immediately after dropping it under my tongue instead of meditating beforehand. After several minutes, I swallowed what was left and continued practicing.

This session occurred late in the evening, so I set up my meditation cushion next to my bed. I began the meditation sitting up while wearing a blindfold. The experience I recorded here took place during an hour or so of sitting, after which I went to bed to meditate lying down until I needed to fall asleep.

Ten to fifteen minutes later, I noticed a change in my perception. My body felt more comfortable and settled as I sat cross-legged on my cushion. This was important to note because many meditators, especially beginners, struggle with pain and discomfort even when sitting in a chair. For some, the hurdle is too great, causing them to give up on meditation altogether.

The next thing I noticed was my thoughts had significantly slowed down. This allowed me to make better contact with them. But the contact had a slippery quality to it. I had to strike a careful balance between observing a thought and hanging on to it. Of course, this balance applies to meditation even without the use of substances.

The thoughts, emotions, and memories had what I would describe as "softer edges" to them. I realized that I sometimes have an adversarial or defensive attitude toward my conceptual mind during practice. The tincture shifted my perception in such a way that the thoughts were no longer a threat. Or was it that I became less aggressive?

During substance-free meditation, thoughts seem to have a one-and-done quality to them. They come and go and therefore can't be re-experienced. But with the tincture, it seemed like I was able to "rewind" a thought if I wanted to.

This was possible partly because the thought velocity was significantly reduced. Earlier, I mentioned how thoughts had a slipperiness to them, which would make the ability to rewind them seem paradoxical.

Although academics and researchers may have a problem with this idea, I'm sure many long-term meditators are perfectly fine with it. Ambiguity and paradox are familiar themes to those who spend years investigating consciousness.

I realized why some people might consider using cannabis with meditation. It can accomplish some of the same goals as ketamine-assisted therapy for trauma work.

Cannabis might aid in processing what would normally be a painful and triggering memory because of its potential to slow things down, reduce defensiveness, soften the imagery, and make it possible to rewind and replay it. This way, the client can process the memory, understand its effect on their present life, and gradually release its hold, all without being retraumatized during the session.

Cannabis with Meditation and Psilocybin

Specific to mind training, cannabis offers the opportunity to investigate the nature of mind by observing the transition from a sober to a non-sober state. Various traditions have their way of doing this, and it's also taught in the *Path's* online meditation program. The training begins by deeply observing one's thoughts as well as differentiating them from fundamental awareness.

Going deeper, the meditator investigates which aspects of consciousness are conditioned by cause-and-effect, and which, if any, are unconditioned. Put simply, the meditator inquires, "Which part of my mind changes from moment to moment, and which part is beyond causes and conditions? Is any part of me unaffected by change?"

Before you, the reader, attempt a conceptual, perhaps doctrinal response to this question, you should know it's not about coming up with an answer.

Transformation comes from the *experience of looking*, of observing the mind during meditation to see what can be seen. Transformation occurs by carefully repeating this investigation while in a state of meditation over years, if not an entire lifetime.

Much like a psychedelic experience, the insights gained cannot be put into words. That's why coming up with a clever answer to the question, "What is the unconditioned mind?" is worthless.

This extremely subtle technique can be applied during transitional states such as falling asleep, dreaming, becoming sick, becoming sexually aroused, sneezing, and orgasm.

One can even apply the training during the final transition, death, which, in some traditions, is the whole point.

As the ancient inscription on the door of St. Paul's monastery at Mount Athos says, "If you die before you die, you will not die when you die."

Meditation, in a way, is preparation for death. And since death is a transitory state, we can prepare for it by meditating during other transitory states, including feeling the effects of cannabis, psilocybin, and other elixirs on one's state of being.

Training this way, we come to understand the parts of ourselves that we must surrender not only at the time of death but on a day-to-day basis. This is what it means to let go. This, it has been said, is how to free oneself from suffering.

Part Two: an anecdote with vaping

In this instance, I prepared around a third of a gram of organic cannabis flower by using my fingers to pulverize it. Then, I loaded it into my **dry herb vaporizer** (the Davinci IQ2)[42]. Just like psilocybin, the weight of cannabis doesn't mean much without additional information.

Along with a person's sensitivity to it, one should know the THC concentration of their cannabis.
I looked at the label and saw that my Purple Punch strain had a THC concentration of 23%. By multiplying that by 0.3 grams, I determined I would be vaping 69 mg.

By knowing this, I was prepared for a much stronger experience than the one with only 35 mg taken as a tincture. It had been a long time since using it, so just like before, I had no tolerance built up.

After loading my vaporizer, I took it to my meditation space. I sat down, put on my blindfold, and set my timer for thirty minutes. My goal was to settle my mind and develop my concentration before vaping. This way, I'd be able to investigate my mind as it transitioned from one state to another.

My timer went off and it was time to vape. All I needed to do was press the power button five times rapidly, at which point it began heating up. I didn't have to remove my blindfold or interrupt my practice to do this. I continued meditating while holding the vaporizer in my lap until several

---

[42] https://davincivaporizer.com (I am not an affiliate for this or any other resource in this book. I'm only sharing what equipment and resources I use).

Cannabis with Meditation and Psilocybin

minutes later when it vibrated, indicating it had reached the proper temperature for me to inhale the vapors.

Path of the Golden Teacher

    I took multiple drags from the vaporizer over several minutes until I was certain I'd used all the cannabis, and then I set it down to the side. I had kept my blindfold on the whole time. I had already set my watch to chronograph mode so I could track how long my meditation would last from that point.

    A couple minutes later I felt my heart rate increase. It became so strong that I could feel it pulsing in my chest. I also felt parts of my body becoming warm and fuzzy, such as the tops of my hands, elbows, and parts of my thighs.

    The benefit of wearing a blindfold is I also noticed the very start of increased phosphene[43] activity behind my eyelids. It started with what looked like a single photon blipping in and out of my vision, and it was red. A tiny red spark. Then my vision was flooded with grayish-white phosphenes. Eventually, they included other colors, but they were extremely muted, like faint pastels.

    Meanwhile, my body had become quite comfortable in my sitting position, just as it had during the session with the tincture, only more so. And when I did move, the sensation was significant. If I didn't move, my body and mind felt sober. But as soon as I did move, I felt inebriated. This encouraged me to enjoy my pain-free posture as much as I could by remaining still so I could go further inward.

    Over time, the phosphenes were replaced first by geometric shapes and then by whole images from everyday life. Animals, people, natural and manufactured elements, all kinds of things. They were constantly in motion, morphing from one shape to another beyond my control and apart from my intention. "I," my conscious self, had nothing to do with the images arising in my mind's eye.

    Like the initial phosphenes, the images appeared extremely muted. I would guess $1/100^{th}$ of the luminosity of

---

[43] If you don't know what phosphenes are, close your eyes in a dark room and gentle press or rub them until you see grayish-white dots or patterns amidst the darkness behind your eyelids.

Cannabis with Meditation and Psilocybin

the hallucinations produced by psilocybin or LSD. I think the only reason I noticed them was because I intentionally looked for them while meditating. For many people, cannabis is used in an *exteriorized* way, such as while socializing with others, looking at scenery, or dancing. With a user's attention directed at external phenomena, that person could completely miss the subtle activity happening behind the mental curtain.

But I was using it in an *interiorized* way, directly looking within while blocking out external light with a blindfold in a darkened room.

I realized why I'd never become a regular cannabis user. Whenever I'd used it before (always in a social, exteriorized context), I felt "off" and agitated. Now I understand why. It's not because I was high. It was because I was in a mildly hallucinatory state and *didn't know it.*

Something was happening inside that I was ignoring because I looked outward instead of within. Some part of me must've noticed enough to produce the agitation, but my conscious mind was clueless. Now it made sense. In those prior attempts to enjoy cannabis, I'd used it in a way inappropriate for my constitution and personality.

As with my other anecdotes, I don't mean to generalize these ideas. My experience may not apply to you.

There were changes to my auditory experience as well. Several airliners flew overhead throughout the session. They sounded much louder than they normally do. I was able to perceive some of the sound waves' higher and lower frequencies, ones which are normally beyond my hearing range. It was quite pleasurable, a richer sound experience than usual.

My mind also produced auditory hallucinations from within, such as people's voices. (I sometimes experience this in substance-free meditation.) But everything was extremely brief. Moment by moment, the appearances evolved without any volition on my part. My consciousness was divided in two. My mind as thoughts and hallucinations was in constant flux while my deeper awareness, playing the role of observer, witnessed everything.

I spent a substantial amount of the session meditating this way, simply watching the ever-changing appearances behind my eyelids and inside my mind. I realized the images were often matched with language-based concepts. It seemed like on a very deep level, every word-thought I had was originated by a picture.

If I paid close enough attention, I could almost discern the ultrafast transition of an image into a word. Is that how our brain works? Do we always begin a thought as a subconscious picture, and end it as a conscious language-based concept?

I've heard of this in the context of hypnosis and neurolinguistic programming. But to experience it in meditation with the help of cannabis was intriguing. Eventually, the session went even deeper.

After further observation, my mind became stroboscopic. Millisecond by millisecond, the thoughts and images flashed into and out of existence:

> millisecond 1: appearance/thought
> millisecond 2: nothingness/non-existence
> millisecond 3: repeat

Instead of flowing like an everchanging-yet-constant river, my thoughts became like subatomic particles popping in and out of existence at a nearly indistinguishable rate.

And what of fundamental awareness, was that flickering too? And what does that imply about the nature of selfhood? I will stop here and let you find out for yourself. Hearing about these experiences doesn't change a person. You must find out for yourself while meditating (with or without a psychedelic) and see how the experience strikes you in your bones.

Cannabis with Meditation and Psilocybin

It's important to stress the fact that I was able to perceive my mind this way because of my prior meditation training. I don't think I could have had this kind of experience just by vaping cannabis and sitting down without at least some instruction in and practice of looking at my mind for extended periods.

Although there were hallucinations, the psychedelic effect of cannabis was devoid of the emotional tone typical of psilocybin and LSD. I didn't receive any life-changing insights or spiritual messages, or revisit events from earlier in my life.

I meditated this way sitting up for an hour and forty minutes, then continued meditating while lying down for another hour. Then I got up and did chores around the house while the cannabis' effect receded over a couple more hours.

I suspect using cannabis this way might be good training wheels for someone interested in exploring psilocybin. It's not the same experience, but it's mild enough for dipping one's toes into the psychedelic pool before diving into the deep end.

For regular cannabis users using the *Path's* online guided meditation program, I'd recommend pausing their usage. Instead, save it for the completion of each of the series in the program.

For example, it can take nine weeks to complete the Foundational series if you meditate every day. You might wait until Week 9 to combine cannabis with one of the meditations from that series to see what you learn from it. If that's too long for you to wait, then see if you can limit it to once every two weeks if not once a month.

I recommend **not** using cannabis during your regular meditation practice. Daily meditation should be practiced with an attentive and alert crystal-clear mind. Reserve meditating with cannabis for periodic usage only. If you must use cannabis daily, then try to meditate before your first use of the day, or anytime when you're not under the influence.

Contrasting thoughts, emotions, and awareness in both states of consciousness will help investigate the nature of your mind.

But the vast majority of your meditation training should be substance-free.

For those interested in learning about using cannabis for psychological healing, I recommend Daniel McQueen's book, *Psychedelic Cannabis: Therapeutic Methods and Unique Blends to Treat Trauma and Transform Consciousness*.

For dealing with illness and pain, and improving wellness, see Benjamin Caplan's book, *The Doctor Approved Cannabis Handbook: Reverse Disease, Treat Pain, and Enhance Wellness with Medical Marijuana and CBD*.

JOURNEYING WITH DMT

DMT (*N*, *N*-Dimethyltryptamine) is a molecule structurally similar to psilocybin. It's probably best known as the main active compound in ayahuasca. Ayahuasca is consumed as a brew during Amazonian indigenous rituals which can last several hours, often performed overnight.

It's common for ayahuasca use to result in *purging* through vomiting and diarrhea, which traditional ayahuasca shamans sometimes regard as a sign of cleansing.

The prospect of purging and the default adoption of spiritual beliefs and rituals outside of one's daily worldview can deter a person from participating in ayahuasca rituals.

Fortunately, there is another way to experience a journey with DMT. This involves vaporizing and inhaling a minute amount of DMT crystals which have been extracted from plant matter.

A light dose can produce open-eyed visual hallucinations and an elevated mood. A heavier dose can include more aspects of a complete psychedelic experience. A large dose will produce an experience called *breakthrough*.

Also, any amount of DMT can produce undesirable effects like fear, confusion, sleeplessness, and existential angst. It can pose the same risks listed in the chapter *Contraindications for Psychedelics* in Part Two.

In the breakthrough experience, the journeyer feels like they've been transported to another reality. It's common to lose motor function, making it difficult to move. One should be prepared to lie down for safety immediately after inhaling vaporized DMT.

The DMT journey is brief, only lasting several minutes. This is why some people refer to it as the "businessperson's trip."

From the journeyer's point of view, however, it can feel as if they've been gone for much, much longer. During that time, they can experience a variety of environments which are typically hyper-geometric and brilliantly colorful. It's also possible to experience encounters with various types of otherworldly beings.

One may experience a loss of personal boundaries or of one's whole identity. I'll describe losing mine in the chapter *My Journey with DMT*.

When the journey finishes, one feels completely sober and clearheaded, as if being reset or rebooted.

No matter what occurs during the journey, you will be left with a lot to digest over the following days, or longer.

DMT can be purchased in the form of a vaping pen or cartridge. In this delivery system, the DMT is mixed into a liquid such as vitamin E acetate or propylene glycol. However, there exist serious concerns that inhaling these compounds can lead to lung damage.

Another risk from buying a vaping pen or cartridge is there's no way to verify what substances it contains.

In the spirit of harm reduction, I've included the next two chapters for those who are interested in using DMT.

Journeying with DMT

The very next chapter will show you how to extract DMT in the comfort and safety of your home.

The chapter after will show you how to vaporize the crystals. This way, you can avoid sourcing your DMT from strangers or risking your lung health by inhaling potentially dangerous additives from pens and cartridges.

Be aware the contraindications for psychedelics discussed in Part Two also apply to DMT, including the legal considerations.

CAUTION

Although most psychedelics are not physically addictive[44], the short duration of the DMT journey and its perceived convenience may promote *psychological* addiction and abuse.

Even if you don't intend to have a breakthrough experience, it's difficult to predict what dose will produce that effect for each person. Thus, it's possible to have an *unintended* breakthrough causing you to lose control of your body and become extremely vulnerable.

This is especially dangerous when using a torch lighter with a dab rig or a pipe. The journeyer should never handle the lighter themselves, leaving that task to their sitter. This will be discussed more in the chapter *How to Use DMT*.

---

[44] Ketamine, a dissociative anesthetic with some hallucinogenic properties can be physically addictive, unlike psilocybin, LSD, and DMT. See https://americanaddictioncenters.org/ketamine-abuse.

HOW TO EXTRACT DMT

Overview

This guide will show you how to extract DMT from 100 grams of Mimosa hostilis root bark (MHRB). Other plant sources, such as Acacia confusa, can also be used. There are various extraction methods. The method shown here is called Acid to Base, or A/B. With it, acid (distilled white vinegar) is added to the MHRB and given time to break down the plant matter.

Then, sodium hydroxide (also known as lye or caustic soda) is added to the mixture to raise the pH to base levels. This breaks down the plant matter further to free the DMT molecules.

After sufficient time has passed, naphtha (a petroleum-based solvent) is added to the mixture, which is then warmed until "hand hot". Other solvents such as N-Heptane can also be used but are harder to acquire and more expensive.

With time and continued mixing, the DMT crystals are absorbed into the naphtha, which separates into a layer

How to Extract DMT

that floats above the aqueous root bark solution, much like oil on water.

The naphtha layer is then drawn out of the container using a glass pipette, poured into a glass baking dish, and placed in the freezer.

After 24 to 48 hours, the DMT crystals precipitate out of the naphtha, meaning the crystals solidify out of the liquid naphtha (it doesn't freeze solid like water does) and cling to the glass.

The naphtha is poured from the baking dish and the crystals, which cling to the glass, are allowed to dry. Afterward, a razor blade is used to scrape the crystals off the glass. The crystals are then stored inside an airtight glass container at room temperature, away from sunlight.

The following pages list the necessary materials and equipment and give specific instructions, measurements, and safety warnings for extracting DMT.

You can expect to spend at least two days to complete the process. For safety and to yield as much DMT as possible, it is important to be patient and allow plenty of time at each stage. This is especially true for the stages of mixing with sodium hydroxide, mixing with naphtha, and waiting for the crystals to precipitate from the naphtha while in in the freezer.

MATERIALS AND EQUIPMENT

- **100 grams** of powdered **Mimosa hostilis** root bark (MHRB), also known as Mimosa tenuiflora.

In Brazil, it is known as jurema preta and in Mexico as tepezcohuite[45], and there are several other names for it. Powdered root bark of Acacia confusa can also be used.

Mimosa hostilis can legally be ordered online from vendors like www.mimosaroot.com and is commonly sold as a dye. It also has a variety of medicinal uses.[46]

Whether using Mimosa hostilis or Acacia confusa, be sure to order it in powdered form. If it is whole or shredded it will be very difficult to use and may not yield as much DMT.

The next page shows a packet of powdered MHRB sold as dye concentrate. It also shows the MHRB after being poured out of its packet.

---

[45] There are facial care products available online with the name "tepezcohuite," but it is *not the same* as the root bark powder needed here.

[46] "Herbal Safety." Edited by Armando G Stuart, *UTEP*, www.utep.edu/herbal-safety/herbal-facts/herbal%20facts%20sheet/tepezcohuite.html. Accessed 7 June 2024.

How to Extract DMT

Along with the root bark, you'll need:

- deionized or distilled water.

- distilled white vinegar (5% acidity)

- food-grade sodium hydroxide (also known as lye or caustic soda). This can be ordered online.

- Naphtha. This is available in hardware and woodworking stores as a thinner of enamel and varnishes, for example Klean Strip brand VM&P Naphtha. Naphtha is also sold as lighter fluid (such as Zippo and Ronsonol brands), or as camping stove gas (white gas).

  It's important for your naphtha to be additive-free. The way to test it is to place a few drops on a white porcelain plate and let it evaporate. It should leave no residue behind.

How to Extract DMT

You will also need the following equipment:

- Fire extinguisher. **Naphtha is extremely flammable**. For this reason, you should never use it near an open flame or extreme heat sources. **Do not use a gas stove to extract DMT!** Always have a fire extinguisher with you when using these chemicals and have a companion with you as a precaution.

- PPE – Personal Protective Equipment, including eye protection, mask, and rubber gloves. Working with **sodium hydroxide is potentially hazardous** because eye contact can cause blindness and oral and skin contact can cause severe tissue damage.

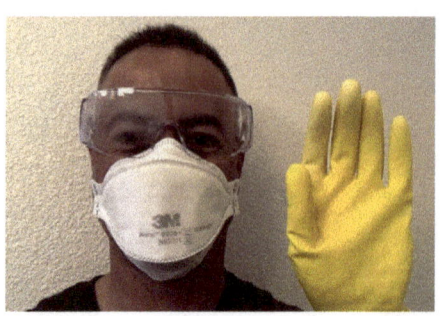

Path of the Golden Teacher

- Two or more glass mixing containers such as flasks (with rubber stoppers), bottles (with metal screw caps), or jars (with metal screw-on lids). At least one container will be used for extraction, and another will be used for storing the chemicals after use.

- Plastic wrap and rubber bands for sealing your glass containers during the heating stages.

- A double boiler or two pots, one small enough to fit inside the other. The smaller pot should be large enough to fit the flask, bottle, or jar you'll use for the extraction.

- pH testing strips, also known as litmus paper. When ordering, be careful to select paper capable of detecting pH 1 to 14. Some pH kits only test a portion of the full range.

- Glass pipette (graduated liquid dropper) with rubber bulb. The one pictured later in this chapter is a 10 ml pipette.

- large funnel, ideally stainless steel

- clear baking dish with lid, paper coffee filter, cup.

- razor blade

- small glass container for storing DMT crystals

- PP#5 (polypropylene) container for weighing sodium hydroxide (since it corrodes most other materials). Stainless steel or glass/Pyrex containers also work as long as your scale can handle their weight.

CAUTION: Do **not** use aluminum with sodium hydroxide because they can react and release hydrogen gas, which is highly flammable. This type of reaction requires water, but still, it's better to use one of the other materials listed above instead.

PART ONE: Creating the ACID mix

1. Pour the dry, powdered root bark inside as glass mixing container such as a flask (with rubber stopper), a bottle (with screw cap), or jar (with lid). The container should be large enough to have several cups of liquid added to it.

2. Add 1 cup of deionized or distilled water to make it wet. If you use a different amount of water, record exactly how much you added because you'll need that measurement for neutralizing the mix in Part 8.

3. Add 1.5 cups of white vinegar and mix it in. Note the dark red hue of the mix.

4. Draw out a drop of the mixture using the glass pipette. Drip it onto a pH strip to determine the mixture's acidity. It should measure a pH of 1 to 2. If it's higher than that, add another half-cup of vinegar and repeat this part. 1.5 cups of vinegar are usually sufficient to reach the necessary acidity.

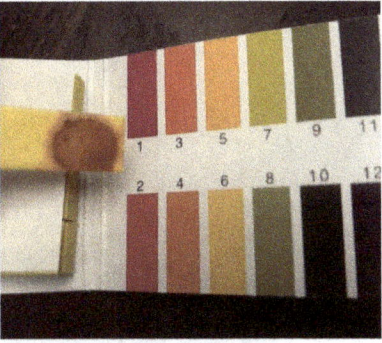

5. Heat the container in a double boiler on LOW for 3 hours. It should be **no hotter** than "hand hot."

   For safety, seal the container with plastic wrap and a rubber band to allow for expansion due to heat.

   Swirl or stir the mixture every twenty minutes because it tends to separate and needs to be recombined.

How to Extract DMT

6. After 3 hours, allow it to cool completely. It's alright to simply turn off the heat and let it sit overnight. You can continue with Part Two the following day.

PART TWO: Turning the mix into a BASE

1. Put on your PPE – your eye protection, mask, and gloves. Also, wear a long-sleeved shirt to prevent the sodium hydroxide from accidentally contacting your forearms.

2. Weigh out 48 grams of sodium hydroxide using a stainless steel spoon and a PP#5 plastic, stainless steel, or glass container since they won't corrode (see the #5 symbol in the next photo). Be sure to tare the scale (zero it out) after putting the empty container on it.

   The general formula is to add is 80 grams of sodium hydroxide per 1 liter (4.2 cups) of liquid.

   Assuming you used **2.5 cups of liquid** in Part One (1 cup of water plus 1.5 cups of vinegar), you'll need **48 grams** of sodium hydroxide to reach the necessary base pH (a pH of 12).

How to Extract DMT

3. Over an hour, carefully pour the sodium hydroxide into the flask <u>one spoonful at a time</u> and swirl to mix after each spoonful. **Wait several minutes in between each spoonful to allow the mix to cool down since sodium hydroxide releases *extreme heat* when combined with water.** Your glass container needs to be strong enough to tolerate this heat.

If you artificially cooled your container down after Part One, such as by refrigeration, allow it to come to room temperature before adding the sodium hydroxide or you risk breaking the glass through temperature shock.

While adding the sodium hydroxide, you'll notice the mixture first become dark gray then black as it reaches a base pH.

The next image shows the necessary **pH of 12** has been reached. Compare it to the litmus test used after creating the acid mix.

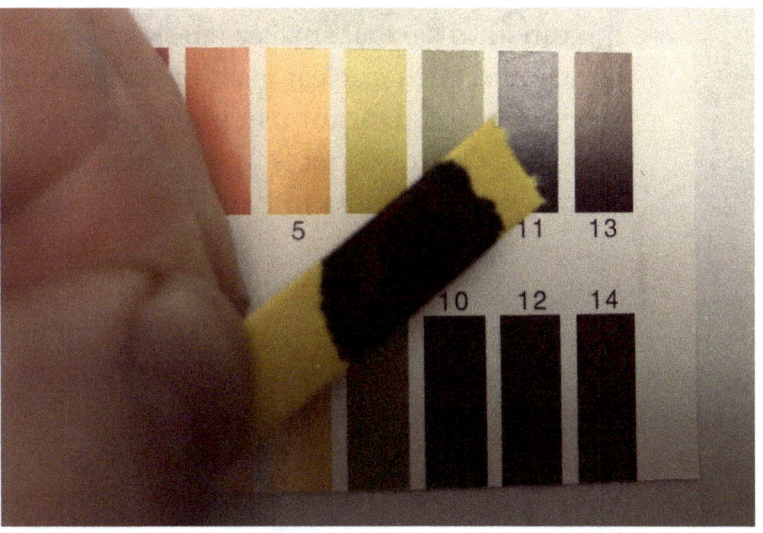

4. After all the sodium hydroxide has been added, mix it well, then let it sit at room temperature for 3 hours.

5. While waiting, put your container of naphtha in the freezer to cool it down. This will greatly reduce the fumes when using it in Part Three.

PART THREE: Combining with naphtha

1. Make sure there are no open flames or sources of sparks in your workspace whenever dealing with naphtha.

2. You can either continue working with the large container you used for Parts 1 and 2 or pour the mixture into several smaller (and narrower) containers, such as clear glass beverage bottles with screw-on caps. **Do not use plastic bottles.** The narrower the container is, the easier it will be to draw out the naphtha in Part Four.

3. Pour enough naphtha into your chosen container(s) to create a layer of 2 to 3 inches on top of the "aqueous" layer (the base mixture). **Naphtha will behave like oil on water.** Leave enough empty space in the bottle for the mixture to expand upward without spilling out when being heated.

4. Seal your container with the rubber stopper (if using a flask) or screw cap (if using a beverage bottle). Shake the mixture vigorously to spread the naphtha throughout the aqueous solution as much as possible.

    CAUTION!!: <u>Every time</u> you remove or replace the rubber stopper or screw cap, and every time you swirl or shake the container, use your personal protective equipment (eye protection, mask, gloves) in case of accidental spraying.

5. Remove the stopper or screw cap and replace it with plastic wrap and a rubber band to allow for expansion while heating the mixture.

   Place the container in a double boiler to heat it. **It only needs to be "hand hot."** Too hot is dangerous. The heat will help the naphtha absorb the freed DMT molecules.

   DO NOT USE A GAS STOVE, or the fumes will catch on fire. If necessary, you can use a crock pot.

   THE SAFEST OPTION is to fill your sink with very hot tap water and set the container in it. Whenever the water in the sink becomes lukewarm, let it drain out and refill the sink with hot water.

   The following photo shows a bottle and canning jar side by side inside the double boiler.

How to Extract DMT

6. Every 20-30 minutes, **put on your personal protective equipment**, remove the plastic wrap, put the stopper or screw cap back on, and swirl or shake the mixture. **<u>Do not shake it if it's too hot.</u>** Instead, swirl the bottle, or slosh it gently, or use a glass stirring rod.

The naphtha will have separated from the aqueous solution and settled on top. It needs to be redistributed throughout the solution to absorb even more DMT.

After swirling or sloshing the container, replace the plastic wrap and put it back in the double boiler (or sink) to warm up again.

CAUTION!! If the solution is too hot, *shaking* it before it has cooled down enough can cause it to blow off the rubber stopper, bottle cap, or lid. It will violently spray the solution all over the room and probably contact your eyes, mouth, and skin.

Imagine shaking a bottle of champagne and popping the cork, causing the champagne to spray everywhere.

I made this mistake of shaking the mixture when it was too hot once. I had to repaint the whole kitchen because the spray had stained every wall and the ceiling too.

I'm lucky none of it made it into my eyes.

7. Do step 6 for at least one hour. The longer you do this process, say for 2 or 3 hours, the more time the naphtha will have to absorb the DMT from the aqueous solution.

8. After your last time sloshing or swirling it, **let it sit for as long as it takes for all the naphtha to separate from the aqueous solution, which could take several hours**. It's easiest to let it sit overnight. Room temperature is fine.

After the clear naphtha has settled on top of the dark aqueous solution, look at it carefully. If you see tiny dark specks moving inside the naphtha layer, give it more time to settle. This occurs when the mixture is still warm and unseparated.

Using naphtha that contains aqueous particles will lead to dirty DMT crystals, so be sure the naphtha has finished settling and the solution is at room temperature before moving on to Part Four.

9. Place your empty baking dishes inside your freezer so they cool down in preparation for Part Four.

Pictured below are a flask showing the naphtha separating from the aqueous layer, a flask after being gently sloshed to combine the naphtha and aqueous solution (note the rubber stopper used while sloshing), and the flask with plastic wrap being warmed in the double boiler.

PART FOUR: Drawing out the naphtha

1. Once the naphtha layer is clear of any aqueous solution, remove the baking dish from the freezer and place it on your workspace next to the liquid.

2. Put on your personal protective equipment in case of spills.

3. Squeeze the bulb on the pipette to create negative pressure, then insert it so it only penetrates clear naphtha layer on top. Move it slowly to avoid disturbing the dark aqueous layer beneath it.

4. Release the pipette's bulb slowly to draw up the naphtha. If you accidentally draw up any of the dark aqueous solution, squeeze it back into the container. It'll sink beneath the naphtha layer.

5. Squirt the clear naphtha from the pipette into one side of the cold baking dish. If the pipette accidentally picks up some aqueous solution, it'll appear as a dark splotch on the glass. You can easily remove it with a paper towel by tilting the dish so the naphtha goes to one side. The dark aqueous solution will stick to the glass, which you can dab clean with the towel.

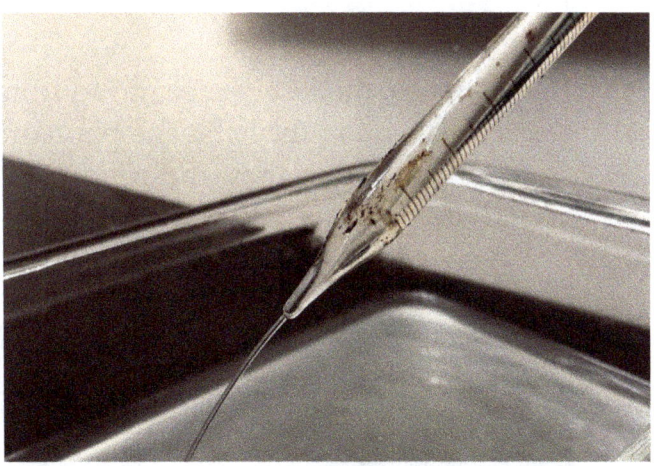

6. Repeat step 5 until all the clear naphtha has been pulled from the mix and added to the baking dish. Don't worry about leaving some of the naphtha behind because you'll do at least one more extraction from the same solution (see step 8 in Part Six).

7. Cover the baking dish with its air-tight lid or plastic wrap and place it flatly inside your freezer.

PART FIVE: Precipitating the DMT from the naphtha

1. Allow the baking dish to sit in the freezer for at least 24-48 hours without being disturbed.

2. During that time, DMT crystals will precipitate out of the naphtha layer, forming on the bottom and sides of the dish. The naphtha will remain in liquid form.

   In this photo, the dish was removed from the freezer, held up to the light, and photographed from underneath to show the silhouette of the crystals in formation.

PART SIX: Collecting the DMT crystals from the baking dish

1. Prepare a container to collect the naphtha you'll pour out of the frozen baking dish. Use a wide-mouthed jar or glass and clip a coffee filter inside of it. The filter should be situated so the bottom is high enough to not rest in the naphtha that passes through it and fills the jar.

2. Pull your baking dish from the freezer. You'll notice small white crystals on the glass.

3. If, when moving the baking dish, you notice many crystals moving or floating around, you'll want to pour the naphtha through the coffee filter to catch the loose crystals. Let the filter air-dry afterward.

The next photo shows the dish after pouring the naphtha out.

How to Extract DMT

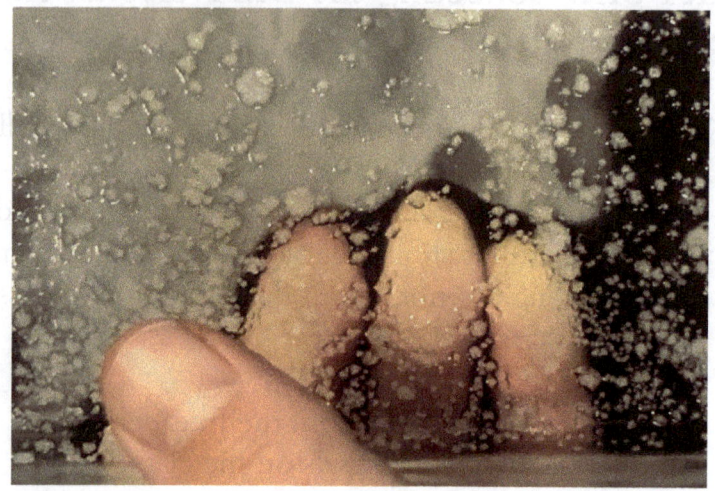

4. The remaining crystals will cling to the glass.

If you skip the step of using a coffee filter because all the crystals are stuck to the glass, you can either tilt the baking dish and use the pipette to draw out the naphtha or pick up the whole dish and **pour the naphtha right back into the container of aqueous solution for doing another "pull" with it later on.**

Doing two or more pulls over a couple of days can yield more DMT, if there is some DMT left in the aqueous layer. If your process was thorough and slow, you may have extracted all the DMT in the first pull, though. The only way to be sure is to do a second pull and see if any crystals form.

The next photo is of using a funnel to pour the used naphtha back into the flask in preparation for a second pull.

5. At this point, your baking dish has no more naphtha in it, and you can see the crystals formed on the bottom and around the edges.

   Place the baking dish upside down and tilted on a plate or in larger dish so that there is space beneath to allow the naphtha to evaporate out of it (next photo).

   The dish should be completely dry of naphtha and water condensation before harvesting the crystals. Give it several hours to be sure all the naphtha has evaporated.

How to Extract DMT

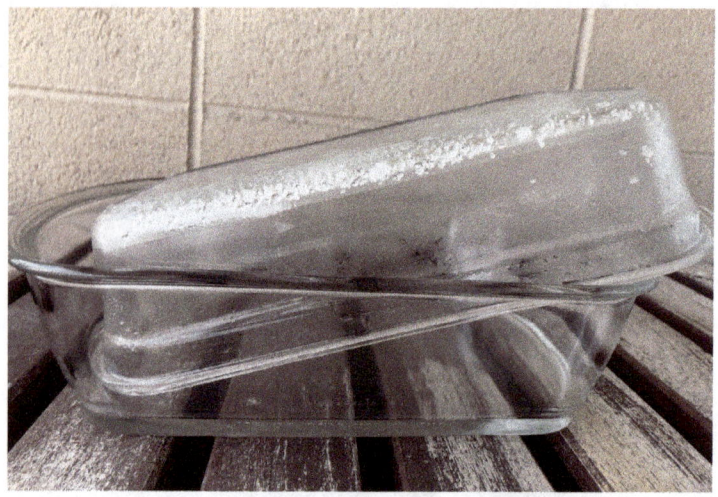

The photo below shows a closeup of a DMT crystal attached to the bottom of the dish after pouring out the naphtha and letting it air dry.

You **should *not*** smell any naphtha in the dish after it's fully dried.

However, there *is* a strong odor like a flowery,

fragrant rubber. To me, it resembles the scent of Linden tree blossoms. Some equate it to the smell of a new pair of sneakers, or new tennis balls right out of the tube.

6. Once the dish is *totally* dry, use a razor blade to scrape the glass and collect the crystals.

    There are usually two stages to scraping the crystals. The first one involves easily scraping off the crisp, top layer of crystals.

    The second one involves the stickier layer of crystals underneath. The stickiness could be plant oil from the root bark. It just requires a little more effort to scrape off.

    The second layer may appear more yellow than white. If you don't smell any naphtha, there's nothing to worry about.

    Some DMT users prefer the darker yellow crystals to the pure white ones, citing differences between the psychedelic experience with each. It's also fine to combine both types of crystals.

How to Extract DMT

7. Collect the crystals from the baking dishes (and don't forget the coffee filter) and store them in a sealed glass container.

8. Repeat Parts Three to Six for as many pulls of naphtha from the container as you want, adding the dried crystals from each pull to the storage container. If no crystals appear in the second pull, that means either all the DMT was extracted the first time, or the instructions regarding length of time and application of heat were not followed properly, probably due to rushing.

    The total amount of DMT produced for the purposes of taking pictures for this book was slightly over 1 gram, and it was extracted in two pulls. The biggest factor in how much DMT is extracted is how much DMT is in the root bark itself, which can vary.
    As you'll see in the next chapter, 1 gram can be enough for 100 light doses, 50 medium doses, or 25 large ("breakthrough") doses.

The image below shows some of the crystals from the first and second pulls from the same aqueous solution. The crystals from the first pull, on the left, are white. The crystals from the second pull, on the right, are yellow. The DMT molecule is polymorphic, so it can appear in different shades of white and yellow. It's possible for plant oils to be present as well.[47]

The best way to store your crystals is at room temperature, away from sunlight, and inside a sealed glass container.

Some people opt to store their crystals in the freezer. If you do so, be sure to let your container come to room temperature before opening it otherwise condensation will accumulate inside the bottle after you open it, melting the crystals and rendering them unusable.

---

[47] These explanations for color variations were found on the forum at www.dmt-nexus.me.

PART SEVEN: Earth-Friendly Disposal

You can reuse your naphtha for future extractions instead of disposing of it. Store it in an airtight container away from heat or flame.

The aqueous solution which you extracted the DMT from still a very high pH. **It is NOT environmentally friendly.**

To neutralize the pH and make it safe for disposal, you need to add enough vinegar (an *acid* solution) to balance out the pH since it is currently a *base* solution.

- Be sure all the naphtha has been pulled out of the aqueous solution before neutralizing it.

- The formula for neutralizing the aqueous solution is to add 1 cup of white vinegar for every 9.3 grams of sodium hydroxide. In this example, we used 48 grams (see part two in this chapter). Therefore, add 5 cups of white vinegar to the mix. You'll need to use a much larger bottle or bowl to hold all the liquid.

- Use litmus paper to test it and **make sure it's neutral (pH of 7)** before disposing of it.

By neutralizing it, you've transformed the solution into a safe, wet mass of powdered root bark which can be disposed of in the trash.

As for disposing of naphtha, check with your local waste disposal company to learn how and when they accept hazardous chemicals.

The next image shows two litmus papers. The one on the left shows the pH with 4 cups of vinegar, the one on the right shows the pH with 5 cups of vinegar. Both are close to the desired pH of 7.

Look at the paper surrounding the dark red splotch where the drops of the mixture were placed on it, not the splotch itself.

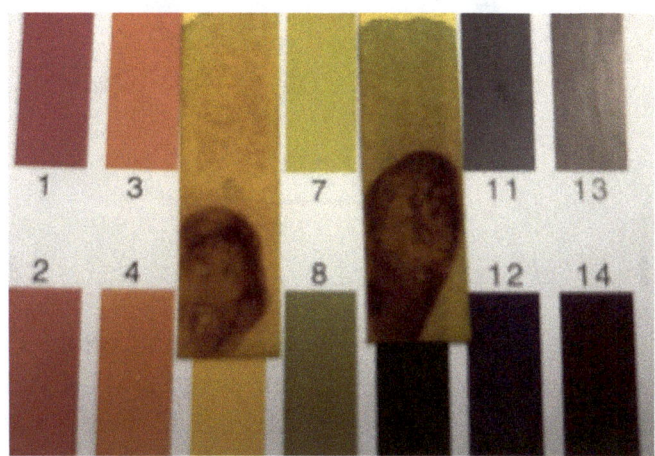

HOW TO USE DMT

Before we discuss how to vaporize and smoke DMT, let's discuss dosages. Only a tiny amount of DMT crystals is needed to produce a psychedelic effect. Still, there is such a thing as a light, medium, and heavy dose. The heavy dose is also known as a "breakthrough" dose, in which the journeyer loses touch with their body and perceives themselves as being in a totally different environment.

Generally, a DMT experience lasts fewer than ten minutes. The effects can begin within seconds of inhalation. The journeyer will usually feel completely normal soon afterward. Of course, they'll process the meaning of their experience over a long period, just as one would after taking any other psychedelic.

The duration and intensity of a DMT experience depend on three things:

- the person's sensitivity to DMT
- dosage
- method of vaporization

DOSAGE

Various online sources list typical dosages with some variation. The following figures are a consolidation of those lists. **You will need a digital scale sensitive enough to measure thousands of a gram (0.001 grams).** These scales can be purchased online for less than $20.

These doses assume you will vaporize your DMT using a glass pipe or *dab rig* (similar to a bong). If you plan to use the "sandwich method" (discussed later in this chapter), it's recommended to add an extra 20% to your dose due to the waste that occurs with that method.

Light dose (recommended for your first time)
5-15 mg (0.005 - 0.015 grams)

Medium dose
15-25 mg (0.015-0.025 grams)

This amount will produce visual hallucinations, including open-eyed hallucinations.

Large dose
25-40mg (0.025-0.04 grams)

This amount (especially at or above 40 mg) can produce a "breakthrough," during which the person loses touch with their body and experiences themselves as being in a completely different environment.

VAPORIZATION VERSUS COMBUSTION

Unlike the cannabis flower (bud) which is combusted (burned), DMT must be vaporized. This means instead of applying a flame directly to the crystals, the flame is applied to the glass container holding the crystals to melt them and produce a vapor. To do this, either a dab rig or glass pipe can be used. Electronic rigs (e-rigs) such as the e-mesh (or emesh) can be used, though they are more complicated and cost more.

USING A DAB RIG

Dab rigs are commonly used for vaporizing cannabis concentrates (dabs) referred to as wax, shatter, and crumble. A dab rig can be used like a bong for burning (combusting) cannabis by placing a regular pipe's bowl in the banger (described below).

Dab rigs can be quite simple and inexpensive to purchase at your local headshop or online.

The image on the next page shows a simple dab rig and indicates three important components:

1. Mouthpiece: where you place your mouth to inhale the vapor.

2. Banger (also called a "nail"): where you place your DMT to heat it with a butane torch lighter.

3. Carb cap: placed on the banger while heating the DMT. This is for a "cold start," discussed on the next page.

> Carb caps are designed to maintain heat inside the banger and to direct the airflow during inhalation. Some caps are striated so they spread out the airflow automatically, while bulbous carb caps are designed to be moved by hand to change the direction of airflow during inhalation to ensure all the contents of the banger are heated evenly.

COLD-STARTING WITH A DAB RIG

For DMT, it's best to do a "cold start," meaning the banger is heated *after* the DMT is added to it to ensure good temperature control and prevent burning the crystals.

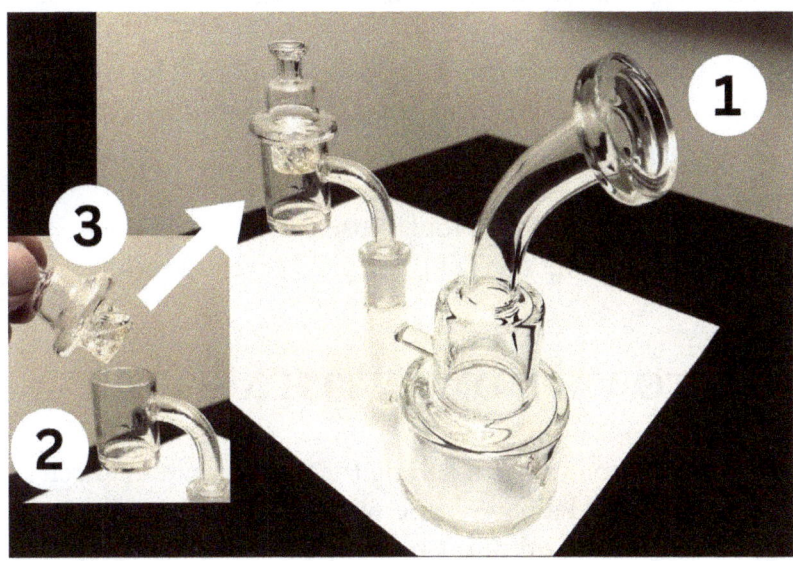

You will also need a butane torch lighter since normal lighters can't produce enough heat. These are available from hardware stores as well as online.

VAPING WITH A PIPE

Vaping can also be accomplished using a small glass pipe, but still requires the use of a torch lighter. At that time of this publication, a popular pipe for vaping DMT is from the company Vapor Genie and is called the "glass Sherlock." You can learn more about it at www.VaporGenie.com/product/glass-sherlock/. Keep in mind that it is much costlier than a simple dab rig, but simpler to use.

Using the search phrase "How to use the Glass Sherlock GVG for DMT" on YouTube will yield several helpful videos.

HOW TO VAPE DMT WITH A SITTER

Since vaping with a dab rig (or pipe) requires a torch lighter, you should **always vape with a sitter who will handle the torch and dab rig or pipe for you.** The last thing you want is to lose motor function with a flaming hot torch in your hand which could set your couch, carpet, table, *or you* on fire after being dropped.

Here are the steps for vaping DMT by doing a cold start with a dab rig:

1. The journeyer should be seated on a couch, bed, or floor where they can easily and safely lie down immediately after inhaling the DMT.

2. The sitter holds the dab rig and torch and is positioned close enough so the journeyer can easily reach the mouthpiece.

3. After placing the crystals in the banger and placing the carb cap on top, the sitter ignites the torch lighter and

holds it two to three inches underneath the banger with the flame pointing up toward the bottom of the banger. Side note: unlike while using a bong for burning cannabis, it's not necessary to fill the rig's main chamber with water.

4. After around twenty seconds, the sitter will notice the crystals melting and boiling. If not, the sitter should move the flame closer to the banger. Once the crystals begin to boil, the sitter should turn off the flame and let the journeyer know it's time for them to inhale the vapors.

5. The journeyer leans forward and slowly inhales through the mouthpiece. The vapor may be clear (preferred) or cloudy-white. The cloudier the vapor is, the harsher it will be to inhale. Cloudiness occurs when too much heat is applied. The vapor will smell and taste like plastic. It's not pleasant.

6. After inhaling, the journeyer should hold their breath for as long as is comfortable and then exhale, followed by a big inhale of fresh air. Then breathe normally.

7. If, after several seconds, the journeyer wants more, they can indicate with a hand gesture (or by speaking if they're still able) for the sitter to hold the dab rig to their mouth so they can inhale more vapor.

8. If the crystals have cooled off, the sitter should use the torch again to heat up the banger.

9. The sitter should be prepared to safely and quickly set down the dab rig and torch and assist the journeyer in lying down/falling backward onto the couch, bed, or floor (if they were seated on the floor to begin with),

especially if a breakthrough dose was loaded into the banger.

10. The sitter should quietly wait while the journeyer has their experience. They should never inhale DMT while waiting because they need to be completely sober in their role.

11. After the journey is complete, the sitter can offer to hear about their experience if the journeyer feels like sharing. Afterward, clean the banger using isopropyl alcohol and a cotton swab.

HOW TO VAPE USING THE "SANDWICH METHOD"

The sandwich method involves using a regular pipe used for smoking cannabis. First, a layer of cannabis flower is placed in the bottom of the bowl. Then, the DMT crystals are placed on top of it. Finally, a layer of cannabis flower is placed on top of the crystals.

The user lights the top layer of cannabis and gently inhales to vaporize the crystals using the heat from the cannabis burning above it. The user can also keep the lighter's flame above the cannabis to add to the heat.

The challenge is to avoid burning the crystals, which is difficult to do. Therefore, many sources recommend adding at least 20% extra DMT in expectation of accidental burning.

Because of this chance of burning, the sandwich method is quite wasteful. And because of the unpredictability of how much will be burned, it's risky because of the addition of extra DMT which may or may not be vaporized. The greatest risk is to those who want a moderate dose, not a large one. If the extra crystals survive and become vaporized, that could lead to an unintended breakthrough experience.

CAUTION:

DMT is one of, if not *the* most powerful and fastest-acting psychedelics in the world. It demands respect.

Even if none of the contraindications listed earlier in the book apply to the user, there is always a risk to one's psychological health from having a breakthrough experience because of its extreme departure from everyday reality. There is also the risk of abusing it through excess dosages and frequency of use, both of which can lead to psychological harm over time.

Before using DMT, consider becoming acquainted with the hallucinatory state by using psilocybin or other psychedelics first.

RECOMMENDED VIDEOS:

On the YouTube channel *Drugslab* (use captions for English):

- "Nellie has a breakthrough on DMT"
  www.youtube.com/watch?v=HPHNakev2ss

- "Bastiaan smokes DMT"
  www.youtube.com/watch?v=EUhdGiMDYtA

On the YouTube channel *Adeptus Psychonautica*:

- "How to Vaporize DMT for a Breakthrough Every Time"
  www.youtube.com/watch?v=5bj0ILXSZ9E

MY JOURNEY WITH DMT

As I mentioned at the start of the book, my experience with psychedelics was part of a year-long experiment done in 2022 called *The Puharich Project.* During the second half of the year, I experimented with macro doses of Psilocybe cubensis, Amanita muscaria, LSA (from Hawaiian Baby Woodrose seeds), LSD, and DMT.

My task was to complete a series of tests of psychic ability (telepathy, clairvoyance, etc.) while under the influence to see how it would affect my abilities. The reality of psychic perception has been scientifically verified[48], and I've seen evidence for it countless times in my own experience and

---

[48] You might start by reading the following:

Radin, Dean. (2013). *Supernormal: Science, Yoga, and the Evidence for Extraordinary Psychic Abilities*. Harmony/Rodale.

Tart, Charles. (2009). *The End of Materialism: How Evidence of the Paranormal is Bringing Science and Spirit Together*. New Harbinger Publications, Inc.

in the hundreds of hours that I've spent training others to access their inherent abilities.

My final experiment was to use DMT and perform a telepathy test while feeling its effects. I was aware of the possibility of losing control with a breakthrough dose, so my goal was to take a light-to-medium dose so I could retain enough consciousness to engage in the test.

There was a problem, though. The digital scale I had at the time wasn't sensitive enough to weigh at the milligram level. No matter how many of the white crystals I added to it, the screen showed the same amount, 0.000 grams. Feeling pressure to get on with the experiment, I did the worst possible thing, I "eyeballed" it.

I placed the unknown weight of crystals in the banger and let my wife Cierra take over from there. She was my sitter and would help keep me safe. This was my first time doing DMT, and I'd extracted it myself for this experiment.

She ignited the torch and heated the banger. I leaned forward on the couch and put my lips to the mouthpiece to draw the air through the dab rig. I immediately tasted the strange, plasticky vapor. Then, even with my eyes open, the room and Cierra began to look different. I asked her to begin the telepathy experiment right away.

Our plan was for her to sit twenty feet away at the dining room table while I stayed on the couch with my back to her. I had a clipboard, paper, and pen at the ready.

As the "sender," Cierra was to stare at a simple line drawing while tracing her finger over it. It was an image that she'd selected herself and which I'd never seen before. Using her intention, she would mentally send me the image. I was the "receiver," and my task was to perceive the psychic impressions she was sending and to sketch whatever came to mind.

But seconds later, I knew our plans had gone out the window. It only took a few moments for Cierra to sit down and focus on the image and for me to pick up my clipboard and pen. My mind was quickly becoming overwhelmed by visual and auditory hallucinations, and I knew there was no way I could distinguish them from the psychic impressions.

I could also tell I was about to leave the room, so to speak, and enter another dimension. I told Cierra, "I'm in for a full ride, so I'll see you in a few minutes." Then I laid back on the couch, set down the clipboard, and let go.

Just a few minutes passed before I returned, but it felt like I'd been gone for days or even weeks. I asked Cierra to resume "sending," but after staring at my clipboard for a few seconds I could tell I was still under the influence and still incapable of engaging the test.

I was also scared. One of the first things I told her as my journey finished was, "I never want to do that again." I was worried I'd lost my mind, the same way I'd become scared when taking mushrooms in college (when I had no preparation and no guidance).[49]

There were a couple of moments during the journey when I looked at Cierra but could not tell the difference between her and me. I saw her body but wasn't sure if that was "me." I looked down at my own body and also couldn't tell if that was "me." The conceptual boundaries that distinguished me from "other" had dissolved.

During the brief period when I was dissociated from my body, I experienced a completely different environment filled with bright colors and geometric shapes. But still, my sense of self was almost completely absent. In a sense, I *was* the environment. My emotional fluctuations were reflected in how the environment moved and appeared.

Afterward, I realized I hadn't actually traveled anywhere. I was simply experiencing my mind, albeit differently from how I normally cognized it. I've had many real out-of-body experiences before, and this was not that. In

---

[49] The full description of the event and the results of the telepathy test (which was one of my best) are included in my book *Dewdrops of Infinity: Psychedelics, Psychic Abilities, UFOs, and the Puharich Project*.

the out-of-body experience, a sense of self is retained even though it looks and feels very different from being in a physical body.[50]

My DMT experience was more like having a stroke, based on Dr. Jill Bolte Taylor's description halfway through her famous Ted Talk, *My Stroke of Insight*.[51]

Later, I recognized that I'd simply had a bad trip, which these days people prefer to call a "challenging experience." It frightened me profoundly.

But it also gave with one of the most important insights of my life, the value and meaning of having the sense of self made possible by the human body and the sophisticated workings of the brain and nervous system.

Without our boundaries, without delineating between self and other, we can't experience life as we know it. We need separation to feel connection. We need an "other" to share our emotions and narratives with, and to create the experience of connectedness with. This is what produces meaning in our lives. And meaning is necessary for profound happiness.

Boundaries are not limited to our physicality. There are boundaries in time, such as the fact that we grow, age, and die. These factors include separation and loss, which normally follows gain and connection. We can't have one without the other. Life is bitter-sweet, and we can't have the sweet without the bitter.

Like countless seekers, I'd spent much of my spiritual life pursuing a non-self or non-dual type of experience. But I've let that go. I realize that for me, the sense of self and duality is a precious gift.

---

[50] For more details about out-of-body experiences, see my book *Renegade Mystic: The Pursuit of Spiritual Freedom Through Consciousness Exploration.*

[51] "My Stroke of Insight | Jill Bolte Taylor | Ted." *YouTube*, 13 Mar. 2008, www.youtube.com/watch?v=UyyjU8fzEYU.

My death will come in time, but I'm no longer afraid of it. What I am afraid of is of not taking advantage of being "me" in this life, with the gift of limits and boundaries inherent in being human.

I'm aware this message contradicts the teachings of certain religions, but that doesn't bother me. We all have our unique paths, and mine is to live this life just as it is. I used to meditate to escape my humanity, but now I meditate to experience it better.

Thanks to meditation and psychedelics, I reached the top of the mountain. Or at least my unique mountain. But when I got there, I realized everything and everyone I needed was back in the village, down below. Without them, there is no meaning to be made and shared. So, I'm done climbing mountains because I know my time is limited and I still have some life left to live.

Everything's fine, just the way it is.

PART FIVE

FINAL CHAPTERS

REVIEWS FROM THE FIRST MEDITATORS

In case it's helpful for you to decide whether to use the *Path of the Golden Teacher* online guided meditation program[52], reviews from the first meditators to use it are on the following pages.

Several initial videos in the program are accessible without needing to purchase it first, which may also help you decide. The program's pre-registration page has a complete list of all the videos included in the course curriculum.

Review by Cheryl Macchia

Hands down, this is the most transformative and enriching course in self-discovery I have ever taken! This meditation course provides unique and progressive tools for the seasoned practitioner and the beginner alike.

Sean is a masterful teacher. Not only are the instructions easy to understand, but he leads each meditation with a calm, soothing manner that keeps the meditator

---

[52] Find it at www.WisdomWithin.**space**/PathOfTheGoldenTeacher

focused and relaxed. Each session provides the perfect balance of structure, guidance, and space for self-exploration.

The entire course is integrative with each meditation building upon the last. Comparing this meditation program to others I've done, I found it to be uniquely transformative in its emphasis on self-discovery, awareness, and compassion.

While other programs may focus more on specific techniques or traditions, this class offered a flexible approach to meditation that felt deeply enriching and nourishing. People spend a fortune and a lifetime to gain the knowledge provided in this course.

Review by Jill Lowy

I found the guided meditations of the Golden Teacher program to be extremely interesting and profound.

I am a long-term meditation practitioner and through the guided meditations, I gained a deeper awareness of my mind. I have been through many Yogic, Buddhist and Taoist meditation programs in the past and many of them do not deal with the internal phenomenon of thoughts, feelings, and emotions which the Golden Teacher Program does very intimately.

The program gives the meditation practitioner an opportunity to look closely at the phenomenon occurring in one's mind and how to let go of negative thoughts and emotions leading to greater peace & happiness. For example, I could observe in my own mind how certain thoughts would lead to emotional distress that I had been holding on to and not fully aware of.

Through one of the guided meditations of just letting the thoughts arise and not reacting to them, I was able to watch negative thoughts appear & dissolve away. Then I found they no longer disturbed my inner peace.

Reviews from the First Meditators

I also thought there was a lot of variety in the guided meditations, which made them very interesting looking at different avenues of the mind. I never felt bored throughout the program. So, I would highly recommend the Golden Teacher Guided Meditations, I think they have much to offer for new beginners in meditation as well as seasoned practitioners.

Review by Neal Clegg

I found the meditations to be of wonderful assistance in my path of spiritual growth. They continually built upon each other to provide a solid base and then to build and expand my meditative practices and experiences.

The structure of the guided meditations was well laid out and the accompanying audio was soothing. Over the duration of the course, I gained a comfortability with my emotional stability and meditative practices to feel more capable of handling intense emotions as they arose in various situations.

I would highly recommend this course to anyone looking to expand their meditative practice.

Review by Celal Aydemir

Based on my experience of meditations Sean guided in person (this includes ZOOM meetings), I can wholeheartedly say that they were deep, insightful, and full of wisdom.

Sean obviously has significant insight into the human body and mind, and has a skillful and effective way of using these insights to guide the meditators. He uses a gentle approach to present these practices, and it is obvious that the way he guides these practices meets the practitioners where they are, allowing them to be non-striving in the process.

I think the program is worthwhile for anyone, even if they never go on a journey, as it provides a great foundation for self-reflection and growth. I'd definitely recommend it to others.

Review by Dana Baggs

Note: Dana wrote her review by responding to a series of cues sent via email ahead of time:

Question: Were the meditations easy, approachable, or challenging in a good way?

Dana: The meditations were so clear, with step-by-step instructions. Every meditation had a pre-meditation video that prepared me for the meditation. Easy, approachable, and challenging in that I find settling my mind into only thinking about the breath a challenge.

Question: Do you like anything about Sean's style of guiding meditation?

Dana: I especially like Sean's tone of voice, the careful but not slow or boring modulation. I like that the pauses still included background noise and I can feel his presence as if we're doing real-time meditation together.

Question: Did any good psychological work occur in the meditations for you?

Dana: Rather than dread/fear what might come up, take the helm. Stop the meditation or journey at my will and set boundaries with any shadows that arise whether they are mental, spiritual, or physical. Real or imagined, regardless.

Reviews from the First Meditators

Question: Do you think the meditations were good for preparing you for a journey?

Dana: Yes! I recently had a plant medicine journey with a group I have journeyed with for four years. I was able to be "alone" waiting for what was to come up for me.

I spoke to the fire and a baboon shaman appeared and spoke to me with his eyes. I wasn't afraid, rather, intrigued. The approach that Sean taught me was amazingly helpful for navigating "the unknown."

Question: Are [the meditations] worthwhile for someone even if they never go on a journey?

Dana: Yes! For me I was able to quiet my mind and go into my heart.

REFERENCE IMAGES FOR THE VISIONARY SERIES

The images on the following pages are referenced in the online guided meditation program *Path of the Golden Teacher*, where they are explained in detail.[53]

The practices in the Visionary series teach how to experience the same visual phenomena depicted on the murals in the Lukhang, the secret temple of the 5th Dalai Lama, some of which are shown here.

It would be out of context and confusing to describe these techniques to those who lack sufficient meditation training to understand their meaning and implications, so they are not discussed here.

---

[53] Find it at www.WisdomWithin.**space**/PathOfTheGoldenTeacher

Reference Images for the Visionary Series

Sri Yantra, oil painting by Henrique Matos

Source:
https://commons.wikimedia.org/wiki/File:2023_Henrique_Matos_Sri_Yantra_02.jpg

God's Eye by Douglas P. Perkins

Source: https://commons.wikimedia.org/wiki/File:God%27s_Eye_front.jpg

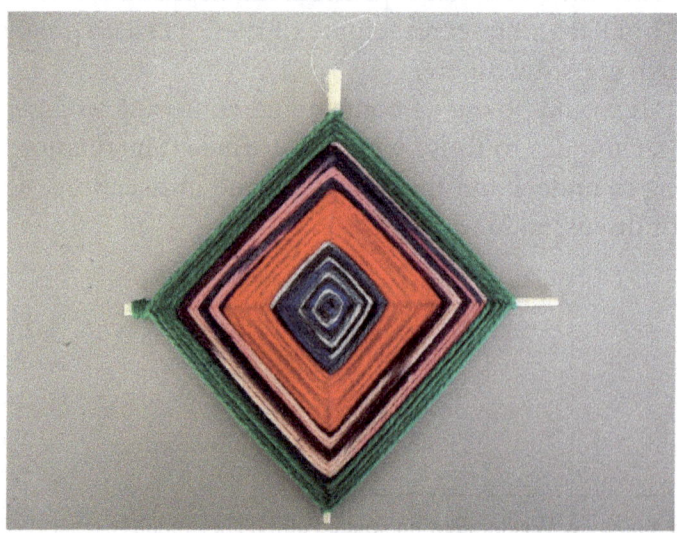

The Helix Nebula NGC 7293 or "The Eye of God": a Gaseous Envelope Expelled By a Dying Star

Source: https://commons.wikimedia.org/wiki/File:NGC7293_(2004).jpg

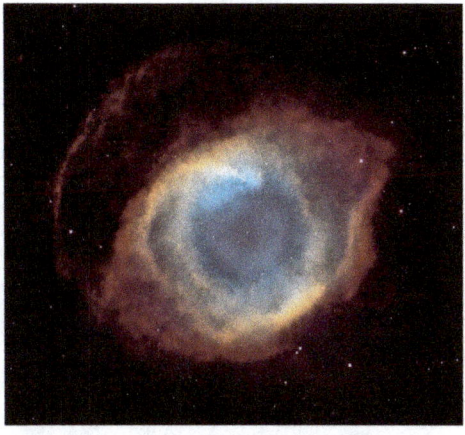

Halo in the Himalayas by Anton Yankovyi

Source: https://commons.wikimedia.org/wiki/File:Halo_in_the_Himalayas.jpg

Reference Images for the Visionary Series

***Fereneze Braes: rock art detail* by Lairich Rig**

Source:
https://commons.wikimedia.org/wiki/File:Fereneze_Braes,_rock_art_detail_-_geograph.org.uk_-_5000108.jpg

***Rosettes at Ormaig rock art site* by Patrick Mackie**

Source:
https://commons.wikimedia.org/wiki/File:Rosettes_at_Ormaig_rock_art_site_-_geograph.org.uk_-_3540725.jpg

Path of the Golden Teacher

Lukhang Temple murals depicting Dzogchen practice

Authors: Wellcome Trust, wellcomecollection.org
Ian Baker, Hamid Sardar, Hon Wai Wai

Source: https://commons.wikimedia.org/wiki/File:Lukhang_mural_9.png

Source: https://commons.wikimedia.org/wiki/File:Lukhang_mural_11.png

Reference Images for the Visionary Series

Lukhang Temple murals depicting Dzogchen practice, continued

Authors: Wellcome Trust, wellcomecollection.org
Ian Baker, Hamid Sardar, Hon Wai Wai

Source: https://commons.wikimedia.org/wiki/File:Lukhang_mural_16.png

Source: https://commons.wikimedia.org/wiki/File:Lukhang_mural_17.png

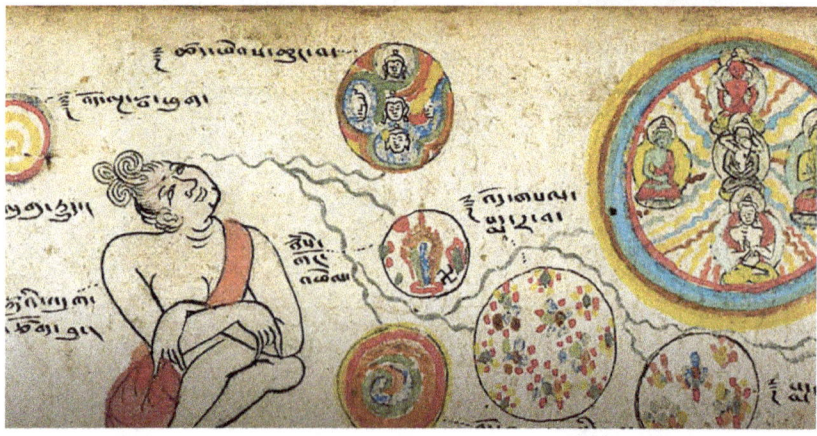

Path of the Golden Teacher

19th century Tibetan thangka of the Nyingma lineage, depicting the so-called phenomenon "rainbow body" of Padmasambhava (center).

Ground mineral pigment on cotton. Private collection. Item number 31903, Himalayan Art Resources.

Source: https://commons.wikimedia.org/wiki/File:Padmasambhava_with_Rainbow_Body_-_19th_century_Tibetan_thangka.jpg

CONCLUSION

I hope this book has empowered you to make certain choices. Should you practice meditation? Should you use a psychedelic? Should you integrate them, and how? And with whom?

But the real question is, do you see the potential here for reaching your spiritual goals? Do you suspect psychedelics are the missing ingredient in your or others' traditions and rituals? Are you ready to empower yourself by practicing spirituality like yogis and mystics around the globe did in ancient times? And the way some of us do today, albeit in secret?

Only you can decide, but now you have more knowledge than you did before which allows you to proceed with caution, intelligence, and the know-how to provide yourself with the necessary elixir.

Hopefully, I left enough space for you to approach this path according to your spiritual affiliation. My goal was certainly not to convert you to my or anyone else's way of thinking.

Of course, I do have suggestions when it comes to practicing the *Path* as it's presented in the online guided meditation program, but that's all they are - suggestions.

As I've mentioned before, you might already have a meditation path or be affiliated with a formal religion. There's no reason to leave it if it suits your needs and makes you happy. But don't be surprised if your journeying causes you to start questioning things. It's only natural and might explain why the powers that be wish to prevent the public from accessing psychedelics.

By now, you should have a better sense of how you might combine a psychedelic journey with your personal rituals if that's something you're interested in doing.

Regarding the few times I shared the spiritual insights from my journeys, please disregard them. You'll have your own insights, and they might differ from mine. I'm anti-dogmatic and think it's important to be clear that your life is unique. What worked for me may not work for you. The lessons I've learned so far (I'm sure there are more to come) might differ from the lessons that await you.

As you can tell, this isn't a reference book or an academic work. The book and online guided meditation program are for those who intend to *do* something with the information, to make their discoveries, heal, find meaning, and seek fulfillment. These are personal practice instructions from me to you.

Or perhaps you're a therapist, meditation instructor, or other helper who wishes to assist others interested in these topics.

Whoever you are, I wish for the best outcome from your good intentions. Writing this marks the end for me, but for you, this might only be the beginning. I'm sad to finish the book, but it makes me happy to wonder what sights you'll see.

We'll probably never meet. But since you're holding this in your hands, I'd like to thank you for being a part of my life, and for letting me be a part of yours.

HOW TO SUBMIT A REVIEW

If you would like to submit a review to support this book and help other people find it, please use this link or the QR code beneath it:

www.Amazon.com/review/create-review?&asin=B0D8H22CFM

ABOUT THE AUTHOR

    Sean McNamara, MA, LPC, lives in Denver with his wife Cierra. He has taught meditation in various contexts for many years. He is a mental health counselor who enjoys paddleboarding, walks in nature, and road tripping across Colorado's western slope to the Utah desert.

Therapy for Colorado residents
www.GoldenMeanCounseling.com

Meditation and Psychedelics Classes and Events
www.WisdomWithin.space (.space, not .com)

Consciousness and Psychic Exploration
www.MindPossible.com

www.ingramcontent.com/pod-product-compliance
Lightning Source LLC
Chambersburg PA
CBHW050551170426
43201CB00011B/1653